& sensibility

sex

& sensibility

steve ayers

inter-varsity press

INTER-VARSITY PRESS
38 De Montfort Street, Leicester LE1 7GP, England

First published 1997

British Library Cataloguing in Publication Data
A catalogue record for this book is available from the British Library.

ISBN 0–85110–892–X

Set in 11½/14pt Garamond No. 3

Typeset in Great Britain by Avocet Typeset, Brill, Aylesbury, Bucks

Printed in Great Britain by Cox & Wyman Ltd., Reading, Berkshire

Inter-Varsity Press is the book-publishing division of the Universities and Colleges Christian Fellowship (formerly the Inter-Varsity Fellowship), a student movement linking Christian Unions in universities and colleges throughout the United Kingdom and the Republic of Ireland, and a member movement of the International Fellowship of Evangelical Students. For information about local and national activities write to UCCF, 38 De Montfort Street, Leicester, LE1 7GP.

& sensibility

acknowledgments

As you might imagine, this hasn't been the easiest of books to write. But thanks to some people it has been easier than it might have been.

Ali Fox, John Goodridge, Stephanie Heald and John Risbridger were all extremely helpful and encouraging – even when they were suggesting how parts should be rewritten. More often than not they were right. Thanks, guys! Thanks are also due to the people who filled out the anonymous surveys which helped me pitch the book at the right level. Thank you, whoever you are.

Most of all though, thanks to Linda for all her help. You're a star!

sex

either of the two categories, male or female, into which organisms are placed; *(inf.)* short for **sexual intercourse**; feelings or behaviour resulting from the urge to gratify sexual instinct; sexual matters in general

sensibility

the ability to perceive or feel; *(often pl.)* the capacity for responding to emotion, *etc.*; discernment, awareness; *(usually pl.)* emotional or moral feelings

(the Collins paperback English dictionary)

1. talking about
my generation

'Our generation loves its pain,
it's marketing it and selling it.' *Tori Amos*

In the last few years we might have seen the death of a couple of cultural icons although, somewhat bizarrely, we can't be completely sure. Two musicians looked up to by both fans and critics are no longer making music. One of them was American, one of them British. We can learn a great deal from both of them. First, back in April 1994, Kurt Cobain shot himself.

As the singer with the Seattle band Nirvana, Kurt had become a reluctant spokesman for a whole group of people who identified with the alienation that his music expressed, echoing what so many felt in their own lives. The band sang of looking for meaning but being unable to find any. Their conclusion to not being able to make sense of life was greeted with a shrug and an ironic 'Nevermind', the title of the album that saw them become massive stars.

Nirvana's lyrics seemed to define so much for so many. Their view struck a chord with a whole range of people. It's by no means just restricted to those we label slackers or grungers. One commentator observes that it's the voice of young professionals listening to Nirvana on their way from the office too.[1] The feeling that there is neither a meaning nor any sense of purpose is a strong one, and it affects people across class and social spectrums. Some of those who feel this way find that they can distract themselves with possessions and a successful career, yet for Kurt it wasn't enough. His suicide note spoke of not getting a buzz from going on stage in the way that Freddie Mercury of Queen appeared to. On the contrary, there were times when it felt as though he was just punching in on a time clock, reporting for work. In the absence of the excitement that he once felt, there didn't seem to be any point in going on.

Kurt's death really seemed to shake a lot of people. Fans all around the world joined in grieving, and the strength of that reaction caught most people by surprise. Looking for a way of expressing how they felt, many wrote letters to the music press. And kept on writing them. The following Christmas, more than eight months after the event, there were still a bunch of letters mourning his death.

'I don't exactly know why I'm writing to you, simply I'm listening to *Unplugged* by my Nirvana, and I'm crying – I don't want to tell you what my life's been since Kurt, my sweet Kurt, is dead.' The writer goes on to detail how he has attempted suicide twice and concludes '... sometimes I really want to die ... Inside my head, I'm dead with Kurt.'[2]

Sadly, this wasn't an isolated letter. Other fans spoke of their struggles with suicidal urges, and so many letters were received that music journalists talked in terms of setting up a support network to put the writers of these letters in touch with each other.

Then, in February 1995, a musician about to embark on a tour of America left his hotel in London and was seen for the last time. Two weeks later his car was found at a motorway service station near Bristol, close to a notorious suicide spot. No-one knows for sure what happened in this case, and no body was ever found. Appeals from family and the musician's band have failed to elicit a response. There have been reported sightings around the world, but what does that tell us at a time when Elvis is regularly spotted in the super-market? The terrible conclusion that no-one wants to draw, but that seems most likely, is that Richey Edwards took his own life.

Richey (sometimes known as Richey James) was lyri-cist with a Welsh band, The Manic Street Preachers. They too sang of the despair and confusion that they saw around them, the album *The Holy Bible* being par-ticularly bleak. Both Richey and Kurt appear to have had great difficulty in coping with the less than idyllic business of adult life. They saw the lovelessness and exploitation they were surrounded by and wrote about it. Both sought relief from these things through the abuse of drugs or alcohol. Richey cut himself too, a way some people try to relieve pressure when they feel it building up inside them. More unusually for a man, he also suffered anorexia, and his openness about his prob-lems meant that some fans identified very strongly with him, particularly those who shared the same troubles. At his disappearance fans were again devastated, with the music press reflecting this. A series of articles under the title 'From Despair to Where' (one of the band's singles) tried to help fans deal with their loss and the sense of uncertainty they were struggling with.

Now one suicide and one unexplained disappearance don't necessarily add up to a culture of despair. But the intensity of identification that so many felt with the worldview of the two singers is worrying, as is the fact that many seem to have had no-one other than the music press to share their deepest feelings with. It seems that the death of Kurt Cobain reflects the way a lot of people feel about life. Before Kurt took his life, the Samaritans reported that the suicide rate in the UK among males aged 15 to 24 had risen by 71% in the ten years between 1982 and 1992. It's a sobering statistic. It's evidence such as this that leads one perceptive commentator to sum up the philosophy of the nineties as 'nihilism'. This almost unpronounceable word combines a belief that there is no belief, with the belief that nothing matters. You may need to read that sentence again! As Kurt summed it up, it's hard to find any meaning in this. Nevermind. We'll come back to Kurt Cobain at the end of the book, but for now let's move on.

On the face of it, these tragedies might not seem to have anything to do with a book on friendships and relationships at the turn of the century. But they do. Deep isolation and a lack of friendship are very apparent in the letter we saw written in response to Kurt's suicide. The author and others like him seem to be left with writing to a music paper as their only option in expressing how they felt. Such a sense of loneliness and a difficulty in forming meaningful relationships isn't confined to those of us who love music, it's more a feature of a whole generation. Ironically, it's the lack of deep friendships with one another that will often cause us to jump straight into going out with someone. Feeling we are alone, we try all the harder to find someone.

One response to our search for meaning is to look for it in a relationship. As individuals we might not matter very much in the grand scheme of things (assuming there is a grand scheme, of course), but we each matter to the person who we love. There's a catch though: because we're feeling isolated, we don't find it easy to commit ourselves to relationships. As a result, we charge into a relationship, get too involved too quickly, and then retreat to nurse our wounds. If that relationship has been sexual, then the results are often devastating. The pain that we've caused each other only goes to make later relationships all the more difficult.

These themes of meaninglessness, alienation and confusion have been written about very perceptively in a number of books by the Canadian author Douglas Coupland. His novel *Generation X* focuses on a generation which commentators have labelled 'X' almost as if to signify that it doesn't stand for anything. Depending on the commentators you listen to, Gen X is the generation born between either 1961 or 1971 and 1981. I'm not sure the exact age-range matters a great deal because the symptoms are ones which all of us will recognize.

Author Janet Bernardi, herself a part of this generation, describes X-ers as having 'problems of stability, self-image, feelings of emptiness, depression, suicidal thinking, fear of the future, and a lack of hope'.[3] It's not a pretty list, is it? Neither is it a complete one. The broader picture is one of a generation looking for community and meaning, but finding neither. These aren't problems unique to X-ers (as anyone who has been through the menopause will tell you), but they do seem to be more keenly felt by this generation than those who preceded it. Though some call them 'X-ers' and some prefer 'slackers' or 'grungers', they're pretty much the same group. It's a generation that I just about belong to, born as I was in the mid-sixties. I know something of the feelings we're talking about. Most of those born in the seventies will know them even more.

In particular, many of us feel let down by the fact that our future has been stolen from us. Coupland describes a generation that is likely to grow up poorer than its parents. Bang goes the myth of material progress! People who graduate, often with decent degrees, find that it can take months to find a job, and then it might be a *McJob* – 'a low-pay, low-prestige, low-dignity, low-benefit, no-future job in the service sector. Frequently considered a satisfying career choice by people who have never held one.'[4] The fact that this is so common is reflected in the joke that does the rounds on campuses:

Q: What do you say to a graduate of (insert university of your choice here) with a job?
A: Big Mac and fries, please.

In reality it's no laughing matter. More and more graduates find themselves in this position, and others are worse off. A university education is no longer a passport to a chosen career, in fact you can't guarantee that you'll walk into a job of any kind. It's almost become an art form to fill out an application form for a McJob – you daren't over-stress your qualifications.

Returning home to live with parent(s) again, if that becomes necessary, makes life even more difficult. (This assumes that there is a family to return to. Some find that their parents have separated while they were away at university.) After several years of coming and going and eating when you feel like it, living at home can feel very restrictive – you didn't go to college for this! Most likely your parents aren't that wild about it either; they were looking forward to a bit of peace. Anyhow, it's no wonder that so many twenty-somethings feel sold down the river, left all dressed down with nowhere to go.

So, as a generation we're fairly hacked off by the world that we're in, a world that we feel has let us down. Little wonder that we're fed up with anyone who tries to offer us the big picture – a philosophy or framework for life, if you like. We don't trust the big institutions any more (political parties, royalty, church, multi-nationals, even charities) and we mistrust anyone offering us easy answers. We've watched thousands of commercials that tell us, however subtly, that we'll suddenly live fulfilled lives once we've switched to a different label of jeans or a new carbonated sugar-free drink.

We know it doesn't work. We're cynical and often rightly so.

This has terrible consequences for us as we go about the business of working at friendships and relationships. It has awful implications for us in the area of sex and marriage too.

The really sad thing is that this cynicism has trickled down into all areas of life and polluted the day-to-day relationships we (would like to) enjoy. Like it or not, we're living in a culture in which people feel isolated, a culture that militates against the very friendships and relationships that we crave. This affects all of us. I know it affects me.

We want to be close to one another, to enjoy the deep and fulfilling relationships that we watch acted out in *Friends*. We want to break out of the vacuum, to banish loneliness, to give and receive love. But we've grown up suspicious of getting too involved. We've been hurt before, and as we nurse the scars, we don't feel inclined to make the same mistakes again.

This has massive implications for the way we live and love; the way that we relate to people, and the way we work out how to relate properly as sexual beings in a world that hardly encourages that. This is particularly hard when, in the search for intimacy, we'll often be tempted to sleep together in the hope that we'll find a soul-mate. What we find, of course, is that sex requires intimacy. It doesn't magically provide it. So we wind up getting hurt again. The search for intimacy, in a world where we feel more and more remote, is one that drives

X-ers though. This raises big questions that we'll go on to tackle later in this book. How do we go about establishing relationships of quality? How do we handle our sexuality in a way that is going to benefit us? How do we deal with the pain caused by past mistakes?

First, though, it's possible that you've read this introduction to Generation X and decided that it says nothing to you about your life. You were born slap bang in the middle of the age-range and yet you don't recognize yourself in this description at all. There could be several reasons for this, one being that you're simply better adjusted than most of the rest of us. If that's the case, please don't get hung up about the fact that you're not that hung up. It's OK to feel 'normal'. More than that, it's desirable. If nothing else though, you should by now have some idea about how a lot of the rest of us feel from time to time. And congratulations! You are probably better placed to work out your friendships and relationships in a more balanced way than most of us.

Most of us need to work at these issues, however. Few of us are fortunate enough to be scar-free after the relationships we've been through, be they platonic or sexual. Relationships can be immensely rewarding and deeply wounding. They can be exceptionally hard work too. But the alternative to putting in that work and being brave enough to get to know anyone at a deep level is the glib superficiality that we too often settle for. It's relatively safe, but it's ultimately unsatisfying and leads to that feeling of having no real meaning or worth that we've been talking about.

That sense of isolation isn't good for us as human beings; we were designed for friendship. We'll look at the whole issue of friendship in our culture in a moment, but first let's look at the opposite: being alone.

'You can have everything in the world and still be the loneliest man, and that is the most bitter type of loneliness. Success has brought me world idolization and millions of pounds, but it's prevented me from having the one thing we all need: a loving on-going relationship.' *Freddie Mercury*

World idolization and huge amounts of cash aside, we've all been there. We all recognize those times when we've felt cut off from every other person on the planet. The suspicion that the telephone will never ring again. And when it does it's someone wanting to sell you double-glazing or to redesign your kitchen. As if life wasn't dull enough already. You know that fear. The fear that the real reason you've no post is *not* because the postman is off with a hernia from struggling up the road carrying all the letters and parcels sent to you. Things are so bad that not even Reader's Digest is sending you any computer-generated post inviting you to win a million pounds. That feeling alone is crippling.

When you get in from your work, you spend evenings on your own in front of the telly, watching actors act out having a life. You watch a soap where everyone in the street knows everyone else, they talk to each other, and they know what is going on in each other's lives. They even seem to get on all right a lot of the time. Just like real life.

Linda and I spent our first year of married life in a terraced house in Swindon. To this day I have no idea who our neighbours were. I only ever saw the people on one side twice. Once was when I was sitting on the doorstep waiting for my wife because I'd locked myself out – again! We had a conversation.

'Locked yourself out, have you?'
'Yes, I'm waiting for my wife to come home from work.'
'Oh well, never mind!'

If your neighbourhood is anything like this, you'll appreciate the dialogue in soap operas. When compared to this rich exchange, actors' talk seems (well, *is*) so much more interesting.

Then one day we returned from a weekend away to find that our neighbours had moved, leaving behind an empty house with a 'Sold' notice posted at the front. We hadn't even known that the house was up for sale. Maybe it never was and they were kidnapped by aliens – aliens with 'Sold' notices at the ready. Maybe we only escaped kidnapping because we went away for the weekend. Sadly, I suspect the truth to be a great deal duller. As a soap opera, Redcliffe Street was a non-starter.

Does any of this sound familiar? In a lot of neighbourhoods, people don't even know each other's names, let alone each other. They rarely speak beyond, 'How are you?' or 'All right?' (Well, actually a lot of the time we aren't all right, but we don't really want to give an honest answer to the question so we say 'Fine'. Imagine the embarrassment if someone told us how they really were feeling!) And while they might like to know what is going on in your life, they certainly don't want you to know what's going on in theirs. All in all, it's the opposite of the picture portrayed in the soaps. You may not be a fan of 'Coronation Street', but Redcliffe Street would have been the nightmare soap, just lots of people walking to and fro trying hard to avoid eye-contact. This lack of community isn't unusual and it's not a phenomenon unique to Swindon, that's for sure.

Research conducted about isolation has shown what we already suspected: it's a lonely planet. Recent surveys[1] have revealed that 25% of the US adult population suffers from chronic loneliness, whilst twice that number (half the population) endures 'acute isolation' in France. In the UK the figure is said to be 14%, which might tell us a bit about our apparent need to be seen as self-sufficient. I strongly suspect that beneath those stiff upper lips there are a lot of us who won't admit to the loneliness we feel.

And the stupid thing is that we aren't supposed to live like this. We were created as relational beings; designed to live with one another and to have friendships and relationships. The Bible has a lot to say on this subject, in fact right at the beginning, in Genesis 1, we read an account of God creating the earth.

We read that, after five days, it's all going very well. On the third day God had separated water from dry land and seen that it was good (verse 10). He then brought about vegetation, plants and trees on the dry land and that was good as well (verse 12). On the fourth day he created the sun, moon and stars, and that was good too (verse 18). The next day saw the creation of the birds, as well as creatures that live in the water. Again the same observation, 'God saw that it was good' (verse 21).

Then look what happened on the sixth day:

> God said, 'Let us make man in our image, in our likeness, and let them rule over the fish of the sea and the birds of the air, over the livestock, over all the earth, and over all the creatures that move along the ground.'
>
> So God created man in his own image, in the image of God he created him; male and female he created them.[2]

This passage is interesting for many reasons. I just want to look at two of them. First, isn't it curious that God uses the plural: 'Let *us* make man in *our* image, in *our* likeness ...'? It seems curious at first, but in the light of other passages in the Bible it becomes clear that God is, mysteriously, three in one: God the Father, God the Son (Jesus Christ) and God the Holy Spirit.[3] Now the Trinity is a difficult concept for us to get our heads around, but it does help us explain why the plural is being used. God isn't talking to himself (though perhaps in a profound sense he is!), and he's not the only one involved in the process of creation.

Here's something that supports this. At the start of

his account of the life of Christ, John states, 'In the beginning was the Word, and the Word was with God, and the Word was God. He was with God in the beginning. Through him all things were made ...'[4] He later makes explicit that 'The Word became flesh and made his dwelling among us.'[5] John then writes an account of Jesus' thirty-three years among the people of Israel. John says that Jesus is the Word made flesh, the Creator God!

Why are we talking about God being three persons? Why is it important? The reason I mention it is because here we have further evidence that God is a relational God. It's a part of his very essence to communicate and to relate, and this is nowhere made more clear than his desire to communicate and relate with those he created, man and woman. The narrative of the Bible makes this point time and time again. From the first created man and woman, through the prophets of the Old Testament, to the disciples and churches of the New Testament – indeed all the way through to this very day – the whole story is of God seeking to communicate with his people. Incredible though it seems, God is interested in us and wants to restore the relationship he once had with us.

This leads us on to the second point that springs from the passage, and it's a much shorter one. Simply notice that man and woman are both created in the image of God. Clearly this cannot mean that we physically look like God. Here in the West we might picture him as a benign old man with a white beard, but that's us creating him in our image. It isn't unreasonable to suppose that a part of being created in God's image is that we were made to communicate and relate, with each other as well as with our Creator. If we read further about the creation of man (because the account records that man was created first) we make an interesting discovery that confirms this. In Genesis 2:18 we read, 'The LORD God said, "It is not good for the man to be alone. I will make a helper suitable for him."'

After all the times that God has looked at what he has created and has seen that it was good, here's the first thing that he says is *not* good – being alone. We're built for relationships. And the solution is a suitable helper, a woman. Now a word to the blokes at this point. Don't get too carried away with the thought that women are your helpers and are therefore in some way subservient to your every wish. Convenient though that might seem to be for us men, it isn't what the passage implies. There are other passages in the Bible where God is described as man's helper, and it would be absurd to think that this makes God inferior to man. It can't be assumed therefore that every time we read of a 'helper' we should think to ourselves that this means something akin to 'slave'. Neither of course does it mean that woman is in some way a God-like helper. As man and woman we have certainly been created different, but we are also created equal. We aren't to lord it over one another. We'll come back to this when we consider marriage in chapter 5.

The weight of biblical material, of which we've hardly

scratched the surface, explains that we were created as people with a need for other people. It's painfully obvious that we aren't creatures made to live alone, as living alone can be so obviously painful. The reason that so many of us remember the times when we felt alone is because those moments are so uncomfortable. It can be no coincidence, for example, that being in solitary confinement is seen as a serious punishment.

We all have different capacities for being alone. Some extroverts seem to have little use for it; some introverts seem to crave it for long periods. Most of us fall into a category somewhere in between. I like to be on my own for fairly long periods of time, and find it quite stressful to be in large groups of people, particularly if I don't really know them very well. But I find it even more stressful to experience the opposite – being alone when I would very much prefer the company of other people. Feeling that loneliness becomes the stuff of *angst*, fuel for some bad poetry – I speak personally here. There's certainly a difference between being alone and being lonely.

As Bryan Ferry once put it so eloquently, 'loneliness is a crowded room'.[6] I like the image that this throws up of people individually feeling lonely in the same place. The truth that this points out is that you can be surrounded by hoards of people and still be very lonely. Physically you might well be one of the family, you might even be married, but you can still feel distant from the people closest to you and feel lonely as a result. In case that passed you by, note again that when we're talking about loneliness we're definitely not talking about the difference between being married and single. You can feel very lonely in a marriage too, as Nelson Mandela famously testified at his own divorce hearing. So if you are feeling lonely, there's no point in rushing into anything in the hope that you'll find a sudden cure. Anyone who equates being alone with being single and lonely should meet some of my single friends – if you can catch them on a night they're free, that is. Essentially, loneliness is an unhappiness at being alone or emotionally distant from those around you.

Lots of songwriters have addressed the problem of loneliness. Sting's 'Message in a Bottle' tells of a man on a desert island who feels as though he's the loneliest man in the world. Desperate to make contact with another person he sends a message in a bottle, only to be greeted with millions of similar messages in return. Now, ignoring the implausibility of the tale for a moment, I think it's almost a parable for today. Lots of us, marooned on our little islands, feeling cut off and alone, making some remote contact with another living person. Nowadays of course the marooned man would have surfed the Internet to make that contact – no-one uses snail mail any more, let alone bottles.

It's interesting that our culture is centred around the individual because so much of what we do actually hinders any chance of decent communication. Student days are generally seen as a time to think through the issues of life, a time to party, do some reading, and join a bunch of societies. I was looking forward to lots of sitting late into the night with mugs of coffee, talking with people about the meaning of life when I went to university. How disappointed I was. Basically, living in halls of residence equalled lots of people living in their own rooms. Occasionally we'd bump into each other in the corridor or the kitchen but even that was unusual. Many people even went to the extremes of cooking in the kitchen and then eating in their own rooms, dinner on their laps, TV on. Things may have got even worse since then too, as residential halls are now often built without a kitchen or any sort of communal space. Other than drinking, the chief diversions are TV (on your own rather than in a TV lounge), music (sometimes on headphones), and computer games.

Now don't get me wrong. I watch TV, love music on headphones, and play computer games to an alarmingly low standard, but the point I'm wanting to make is that these things are generally (though not necessarily exclusively) things you do on your own.

I have met people whose deepest relationship is with their personal computer. There are colleges that are putting a PC in each study bedroom, and perhaps there will come a time when lectures will be provided on line. All very efficient, but it doesn't say a lot for the importance of relationships. We have a need for relationships for the sake of our own mental health and emotional well-being. An important part of work and study is the opportunity that this brings to socialize and interact with others. Half of those starting courses are now continuing to live at home, however, and for students in this situation, developing those relationships is made even more difficult.

If you start in a new town as a student there are probably hundreds, or even thousands, in the same situation, and everyone makes a concerted effort to win friends and influence people. In fact, after three weeks of being desperate to make friends, you'll probably spend three terms trying to get rid of the ones that you're not so keen on after all. You are in a situation, however, where a lot of people of similar age and outlook are all trying to be reasonably friendly and make some attempts at conversation. OK, so the extent of some of that conversation is a bit unimaginative: What's your name? What course are you doing? What were your A-level grades? But at least it's an attempt, and there's the opportunity to move on from there to something a little more meaningful.

For people entering the world of work in a new town, though, it's much more difficult than for students for all kinds of reasons. With the increase in mobility of the work-force, it's often the case that, if you do find a job that suits the kind of qualifications you have, a move is in order. This can be very difficult. The move to a new town might be exactly the sort of adventure that you relish, but if you're making that move on your own, you'll no doubt be feeling rather apprehensive about it. Most people starting work don't have the luxury of starting the same job at the same time as a whole bunch of others. In addition to this, a lot more of us are living alone these days. Analysts estimate that 30% of us will be living in one-person households by the turn of the century.[7] If you live in one place and work some distance away, the feeling of isolation is worse. Even if you work with people of a similar age or outlook, there's no guarantee that you'll meet lots of interesting people or have any form of social life at work. I should know, I used to work in an accountancy office. Although I worked with some great people the workplace was set up so that everyone had their own office. Some mornings the only person you'd see was the person who brought the coffee. Cooped up in our individual rooms, I sometimes felt as though we were battery office-workers.

All in all, it seems that in the world of work the odds can be stacked against you somewhat, and the networks that you took for granted at school or as a student aren't there. If you are working at home, it's time to develop a network of supportive and understanding friends, quick! If you're moving to a new place with a spouse or partner, things may be a little easier, as at least you know one other person in this strange town. It might be easier, but is it easy?

Dave and Alison met at university and enjoyed an active social life there. On graduating they moved to Canterbury, which was useful for the jobs that they'd found. They both had to commute, but no matter, they felt sure they'd soon settle in to life in the city. It turned out to be harder than they thought. I met them at a wedding reception after they had been in Canterbury for six years, and they were talking about how hard it still was to meet people and make friends. Several months later I saw Dave in the pub, drinking with a couple of mates. I said 'Hello' and thought how good it was that he'd met a few people since I'd last seen him. He later said that he'd met all four people whom he knew in Canterbury that night. My wife and I were two of them. It's not as if Dave and Alison don't have any social skills. It's just that it's hard to develop any sort of friendships, let alone the deep ones that you can count on, when you're in a town where you still don't really know your way around very well. And few of us are faithful to any town; we relocate every few years and start the whole process all over again.

By way of contrast, I'm grateful for the fact that Linda and I were in a very different situation to Dave and Alison when we moved to the city. One of the first priorities we had when we got there was to find a church. Now we don't go to the perfect church; they wouldn't have let us join if they were worrying about someone coming in and spoiling that perfection. But we were made to feel welcome, and after some time there we can see that we have made a good number of friends, some of whom we're pretty close to. Friends who have come to visit us have remarked upon this. They've seen the sense of community that we enjoy, and whilst it's nowhere near perfect, there is a trace of the way that it should be. I reckon it would be much harder to get to know people without being a part of a church. For us it's a real God-send. As it is, despite not being Olympic medalists for our relational skills, we've been able to enjoy getting to know a lot of people. It makes living in Canterbury so much more pleasurable. Making friends is far from being the main reason that we made it a priority to find a church when we moved, but it's been an enormous benefit.

Those who study the life of the New Testament church shouldn't be surprised by this sense of community. Although we often enjoy only a faint echo of those relationships in our churches, it's the way that it's supposed to be. In Acts we read that the earliest Christian church stood out for exactly this reason.

> They devoted themselves to the apostles' teaching and to the fellowship, to the breaking of bread and to prayer. Everyone was filled with awe, and many wonders and miraculous signs were done by the apostles. All the believers were together and had everything in common. Selling their possessions and goods, they gave to anyone as he had need. Every day they continued to meet together in the temple courts. They broke bread in their homes and ate together with glad and sincere hearts, praising God and enjoying the favour of all the people. And the Lord added to their number daily those who were being saved.[8]

As I read these words I realize how far our church, in common with most others, falls short of those sorts of standards, and that's because of the likes of me. Here's a community that stood out because it was full of people who looked after each other.

Rather than try to keep up with the Joneses, these

people were feeding them. No wonder they enjoyed the favour of all people! The early church was involved with healing the sick. The disciples took great risks, travelling to preach in public a message that was unpopular with the authorities. Some were imprisoned, beaten or sentenced to death for their actions. Yet rather than shrink the church grew and grew.

A common complaint about the church today is that it is weak and woolly; it doesn't seem to know what it stands for. You could never level an accusation like that at the early church. It knew what it stood for and got on with the job. And the church grew. It was an exciting and vibrant community, and let's be honest here. Hands up, who thinks in such terms when they think of church? Thought not! If you don't think of church as exciting and yet you go to church, take a guess how people who don't make a habit of giving up their Sunday mornings feel. I mention this to point out that the church should demonstrate a sense of community which is *attractive* to a whole range of people who feel quite alone where they are. That's not just down to the minister to remedy; we can all play a part in being welcoming and friendly to people in church. As it is, all too often we come across as a dull bunch who are suspicious of fun. Sometimes that's because we are.

With such a feeling of alienation and loneliness among those moving to new areas, it's hardly surprising that there are people who have more friends, or who at least know more people, through the Internet than people they see face to face.

There you go (I hear you say), here are people making friends across the globe, thanks to the advance of science. Well, yes – and no. I wouldn't want to deny that there are aspects of relationship in this type of communication, but let's not lose sight of the fact that this is just an electronic form of pen pal. There's undoubtedly a limit to the depth of communication going on here, in the same way that speaking to someone on the phone is no substitute for face-to-face communication. Even in the cases of people meeting through the Net and then getting married, the couple have presumably met face to face before getting married. This is partly in order to communicate more fully face to face, and partly because it's not unusual for people on the Internet to lie about their gender. That could be a shock on your wedding day!

Communication by computer screen is obviously never going to be as intimate or interesting as meeting a person. So I'm not convinced that the Internet holds the key to everyone in the world coming together and banishing loneliness for ever. To be fair, I don't think that many would claim that it will. It might even heighten that sense of loneliness.

Where does this leave us, then? It leaves us feeling lonely, wanting deeper friendships, but perhaps unprepared for the vulnerability and openness that they would entail. This might not seem too much of a problem, but as we'll see later it can have implications for the friendships we do have and, beyond that, for the way we relate as sexual beings. All this talk of loneliness

33

probably makes you feel even better than ever! Thankfully, it isn't a life sentence, so let's look at how we can go about this complicated business of friendship, one that can be so immensely enriching.

3. i'll be there for you

CARTOON EMILY

Cartoon Emily, pretty as a postcard
Looks for all the world
Like the world should take a look
She wears blues, yellows and greens
But hides, inside, the cold colours of winter.
Cartoon Emily, secret princess,
Feels as dirty as the new poetry
Espoused on the walls above urinals.

Catch her alone and her drinks are tall,
Deep in thought her talk is small.

She's redrawn herself so that people will smile
And not discover her eggshell heart.
Painting her face to face the world
She secretly fears she's becoming hard,
Cartoon knows she's playing a part.
Yet wanting to be where her new face will fit
She's slashing seats and sucking bus tickets with
   the rest
While laughter masks the anger in her eyes.

Believing her worth is just skin deep
Emily cries herself to sleep.

Battered by blue jokes and white lies
Cartoon has lost the wonder of being Emily.
She's painted herself into a corner seat
Where she wonders about being Emily again.
To be talking talk that somehow mattered
To be considered for more than what she wears.
To have a really good friend. To be loved.
Simple dreams for a girl.

At night, hugging her pillow,
Emily never felt so low.[1]

I'm not a great one for remembering the exact wording
of quotes but there's a Chinese proverb that conveys this
truth: *If you have a good friend in life you're fortunate. If you
have two then you are unusually blessed. And if you think you
have three then you are almost certainly mistaken.* The author
C. S. Lewis hints at the same thing when he talks about
so few of us appreciating friendship because so few of us
actually experience it.

Doesn't that seem a strange thing to say when so
many of us talk to dozens of people in a week: people at
the place where we work or study, people we drink with
or live among? Well, I think we've already pointed out
that there's a world of difference between having some
sort of contact and interaction with someone and really
knowing them as a friend. We might know the
newsagent or the postman or the person at the next
desk, but that doesn't necessarily equate to being a
friend. Friendship is something much more than that,

as implied by the assertion that so few of us experience it. Lots of us are still on the margins of friendship. We're on polite terms with it but, like Cartoon Emily, we still retreat to our homes feeling lonely. Why is it that friendship is so difficult? Why do we have such a problem with it?

Look at it this way. Try making a list of all the things that you look for in a friend. Imagine that you want a friend and are writing an advertisement for one. Apart from (presumably) being house-trained, what are the qualities and the characteristics that you are going to be looking for? This isn't just a rhetorical question; you'll find it helpful to spend two or three minutes doing this exercise right now … Done it? Keep the list that you've made.

We'll think about the qualities you are looking for a bit later on, but first let me point something out. This may or may not be on your list but, without it, the friendship will never develop into anything of any great depth. The person for whom you are advertising needs to be able, and prepared, to be open with you and vulnerable. You need to be able to see what they are really like. Because unless you do, you'll only ever interact on a surface level and won't be able to develop anything deeper. But here's the catch. To be in that kind of deep friendship, where you know another person more intimately, you have to be prepared to do the same. You need to be open in your attitude to that person. Because, if vulnerability goes only one way, you end up with some pretty bizarre relationships – relationships that are particularly open to abuse.

Some people seem to have no problem with this concept of vulnerability. The comedians Mel Smith and Griff Rhys-Jones once made a spoof charity appeal on behalf of people who were born without any sense of embarrassment. Ever met someone like that? I've certainly met one or two people who, with no prompting whatsoever, proceeded to tell me their life history in, shall we say, unnecessarily personal detail. Maybe you've done it yourself. I suspect that I might have. Often when we react in this way it's a sign that we aren't altogether happy with the way we feel about ourselves. That poor self-image is what makes us all the more desperate for other people to like us and affirm us, and so we charge in too soon and reveal too much of ourselves. Awkward conversations follow! We need to issue a word of warning here. When we talk about being vulnerable, we aren't talking about charging straight into a relationship and shedding any inhibitions that we might have. Neither can we hope to have this kind of open and intimate relationship with everyone we come into contact with. That kind of emotional promiscuity is unrealistic and unhelpful, and taken to extremes could lead to all kinds of problems ranging from ridicule to physical assault. There have to be some guidelines to this. We shouldn't expect to have dozens of close friends. There are degrees of friendship, and we should expect that in our lives.

Some Christians I know have difficulties with this

point; they seem to think that being a Christian means that we should be friends with everyone we come into contact with. There's something to be said for this attitude. We should be aiming to include the people who tend to be on the fringes of our groups. Next time you have a party, don't just invite all the people that you like. It's not realistic, however, to expect that you will be soul-mates with all the people you come into contact with. There's no point in feeling guilty about not getting on famously with everyone, but you can still be friendly to all people. Let's face it, it would be physically and emotionally impossible to be best friends with everyone we meet.

People who tell you everything about themselves, without the context of any friendship, stand out when you meet them, mainly because they are the exception. Most of us have the opposite problem. It takes a lot for us to open up to other people. Being the sophisticated creatures that we are, we have developed a number of strategies that we can use to keep people at arm's length and stop them getting close enough to know us well. These strategies aren't always consciously employed, but are certainly understandable. If you refer back to the first chapter, which talked about the sense of hurt and disappointment that so many of us have felt whether we are part of Generation X or not, it's hardly surprising that we employ some defence strategies to limit potential damage (to ourselves!) in our relationships. Having been hurt before, we are less than keen to be put through the wringer in our relationships again. So we hang back in a variety of ways in the hope of affording ourselves a little protection. Let's look at some of the strategies that we might use.

The first of these might be surprising at first sight but is one that we've all seen, I'm sure. For lack of a more professional term I'll call it the *cliquey and exclusive relationship*, and it's a trap that a lot of people fall into. It can be the case between close friends of the same sex, but is often most visible when a couple start going out together.

Couples in this position have managed to let down their defences and found that they like a person and that other person likes them. They've got over the difficulties of the odd misunderstanding and found that they can enjoy an intimate friendship. (I make the whole thing sound such a minefield, but it can be a deeply pleasurable experience, honestly!) Then they live in each other's pockets and are never seen apart again – ever. This is a particular danger if they are in the hallowed world of college or university. Without having any outside responsibility to anyone else, these couples spend every waking moment together, and often sleeping moments too. They shop together, they eat together, you even suspect that they go to each other's lectures too – that's a sure sign that things have really got bad!

Obviously, getting to know your boy/girlfriend well is vital, particularly if you're thinking in terms of spending your life together. But such intense relationships mean that you get to know each other really quickly, and in the thrill and rush of it all you can get swept along faster than you might like. We'll look at this in more detail later, but first let's look at it from another angle. If you recognize a bit of yourself in the kind of relationship I've just described, can I ask you a question? Do you ever still see the friends you used to spend time with before you met Mr/Ms Right? Spending all that time together usually means you neglect other friends without realizing it. Those other relationships will then remain superficial, or at least stop developing. Don't make the mistake of cutting yourself off from those people you were close to before the big romance started.

That might mean that you need to be separate from your significant other for an hour or two every now and again so that you can spend some time with your other friends. This might not be easy at first, particularly if your friends are (understandably) feeling a bit miffed at the fact that they were seemingly dropped once you found the person of your dreams. They might be feeling rather lonely if you were the person with whom they spent most of their time before your great romance. Your new relationship might also have increased any feelings of isolation that they feel if they are particularly concerned about never being in the kind of relationship that you are clearly enjoying. But even though it might be hard work, you should persevere with rebuilding that friendship if it has fallen into disrepair. The balance in and of relationships should do you a lot of good in the long term too. On top of that, if things don't work out between you and yours (hey, I only said *if*!), it would be good to have the support of friends and some company afterwards. And if things go swimmingly, you'll need some friends to invite to the wedding!

The most important ingredient in a romantic relationship, of course, is that the couple are good friends. It doesn't sound wildly sexy and exciting, but companionship is so important for a relationship. Friendship needs to be there as a foundation if a couple is going to weather the storms that will inevitably crop up from time to time. This is why we're now spending time thinking about the business of friendship before we get on to the spicier stuff of sex and relationships. All friendships will be good preparation for a romantic relationship because we're learning the business of communicating and relating to other people. That isn't to relegate platonic relationships to being merely a training ground before the serious stuff of love and marriage, by the way! But if we haven't learnt how to relate to other people, we are often driven into an exclusive relationship in order to remedy the lack of friendship in our lives.

A second strategy for keeping people at arm's length and not allowing the relationship to deepen is to develop what I'd call a *professional relationship* with people. It's a very polite way of doing things, and perhaps we English are particularly good at it. It's dead easy too; all you need to do is be reasonably polite to people and talk about things that are really rather superficial. So we talk about the weather, a car journey, or a soap opera that we've watched, but the conversation tends to be on the level of the factual. If anyone asks how we are, we tell them that we're fine even though life may be falling apart around us, and one of the really stupid things about this is that lots of us do this in church too.

Surely the one place in the world where we can be completely real with each other should be the church. I've already mentioned that some of our friends have commented that the atmosphere in our church is quite friendly. It isn't the case in all churches, is it? You can easily come away from a lot of churches feeling dispirited and without experiencing any of the sense of community that we identified in the early church in Acts. Whatever our particular church is like at welcoming visitors, we can all learn something more about being in a deeper relationship with one another.

It's deeply saddening that there are people in churches who feel that, when they have a problem, the church is the last place in the world where they can talk about it. Why is that? Why do we feel that we have to keep up a pretence that we are coping with everything in life if we are Christians? It can go to such ridiculous lengths that we can then start being unreal with God, let alone our friends in the church.

We only have to glance at the Bible to see that the reactions of Jesus are far more genuine. They are a much better model for the way that we should go about our own relationships. When he was in considerable distress in the Garden of Gethsemane, before he was arrested and put to death, Jesus wanted his friends around to

43

support him, and it's observed by Matthew that he was 'sorrowful and troubled' as he prayed.[2] There was none of the pointless pretence that we sometimes feel we should put on when we're going through hard times. Some of us are too keen to be seen as good sound Christians and feel that if we show how we're really feeling, especially in front of friends who don't share our beliefs, we won't be great advertisements for the faith. As though we are, anyway! So we try, often from the best of motives, to put on a good show because we wrongly think it's the Christian thing to do. When we look at how Jesus reacted to difficulties, it makes some of our pious attempts look very small and pathetic indeed. It's almost as if we think we can out-Christian Christ.

It's no different in the Old Testament. David wrote a number of psalms that are rarely read in our churches because their honesty about anger and grief sits uncomfortably with us. We don't really like the anger with which David writes about his enemies, for instance. Why couldn't he have been more forgiving? Well, David's friendship with God was a deep one. He knew that God knew him intimately already and that it didn't make any sense to write a (dishonestly) polite psalm which didn't acknowledge how difficult things were. It would be daft to accuse David of being unspiritual because he wasn't wearing a pious mask and pretending that everything in the garden was rosy. And the fact that the psalms are seen as the hymn-book of the church should demonstrate that we can be completely honest with God about how we feel. If you remain in any doubt, read the book of Job sometime.

There's a third strategy for keeping people at arm's length which is quite common. Let's call it *serial friendship*. I dare say that most of us have run across this sort of relationship at some time, be it platonic or romantic. The start of a friendship with a serial friend is often deeply exciting. Such people make good friends who devote a lot of time and energy to your relationship; you might be quite flattered that they have paid you so much attention. But after a while you don't see nearly as much of them; they aren't around as much. This can happen for all sorts of reasons. The serial friend might not like to allow other people to get close, perhaps for fear of being rejected. Sometimes it is due to failure to prioritize friendships, and the person runs around trying to be best friends to everyone until he or she collapses in a heap. Or maybe the serial friend is always on the lookout for the next exciting person to come along.

Whatever the reason for the brevity of friendship, if you feel as though you've been dropped, it will feel like a personal rejection. It might even *be* a personal rejection, but if so it's likely to be because the serial friend is something of a perfectionist. Friends like this get close up to a person and then find that there are a few blemishes; you weren't quite the person they thought. Aside from becoming perfect, there's little you can do about it. Until they change, you won't have much chance of developing a meaningful and lasting relationship with them. That's not to say that you should drop the friendship completely, but we often make the mistake of thinking that we can cure someone like this. In romantic relationships we might marry them, thinking that we can change them. We usually get hurt in the process.

If only we were more real with each other and developed deeper relationships with one another, we'd be secure enough to be honest with each other and with God. If we had the kind of concern for each other that we see in the early church, we wouldn't be quite so scared to get involved in the sometimes messy business of facing up to problems and difficulties together. We might not have any answers for a person who tells us, 'Actually I'm feeling terrible, my mother's seriously ill and I'm not sure that I can even believe in God any more', but we can still stand alongside someone who's going through something like that. Surely it has to be better than wearing the respectable masks that we so easily slip on every Sunday.

I'm as guilty as anyone on this score. Once the sermon is over and we've sung a final song, I find it easy to talk to people for a variety of different reasons. There might be people who I need to arrange a meeting with, or pass some information to, or talk to about the football, or discuss the merits of REM's albums with. It all needs to be done (well, probably!), but by doing it I find I've lost the chance to mull over the sermon for a bit and work out what difference it's going to make to my life. (Sermons should do this, by the way.) Good preaching should touch on some deep and personal parts of my life, and if I don't even consider what I've just heard, I certainly won't get to the place where I can discuss it with a particularly good friend. Discussions about music, sport and weather might be a good way of being friendly towards someone we don't know well, but if we stay on this level with everyone it becomes another way of being distracted from the business of building deeper friendships.

And we boys aren't generally that good at opening up to each other anyway. This can be for many reasons. Lots of us were brought up to be told that real men don't cry. They keep a stiff upper lip in a crisis, and whilst we might have feelings, we certainly don't discuss them – that's strictly for the women. Tragically, it means that most men will be far more comfortable discussing football, cars or their jobs than, say, how they feel about a relationship. Now I love to talk about football, but if I only ever communicated in fairly shallow terms about how excellent West Ham United are, I would have no chance of developing a friendship – ever! For true friendship, you need to go a bit deeper than that. Yet the closest that many men will come to talking about a relationship is to moan about someone, and interestingly that's usually because they have been slighted in some way. I heard a classic 'conversation' on the train recently where a man was complaining in great detail to his mates about 'the wife' and the mess that she'd made of the decorating. What really struck me was that the way he spoke about his wife was similar to the way that you might complain about your dog having chewed up your Subbuteo pitch. By talking in such abstract terms with other blokes, we try to demonstrate that we aren't vulnerable, because, let's face it, that wouldn't be macho, would it? (As though we're fooling each other.)

Because of the way that young males are generally brought up, therefore, we find it hard to be open and vulnerable with other men. If you do manage to, then for too many it carries connotations of being wet and a bit pathetic; you might be regarded as a bit of a sissy. The writer Roy McCloughry even comments that a lot of young men are scared of expressing how they feel about each other for fear that people will call their very sexuality into question.[3] This is reflected by Alberto Uderzo, the author of the Asterix cartoon, who has been quoted as saying, 'I'm surprised no one has accused Asterix and Obelix of being homosexual. Their intimacy could be seen as not entirely normal.'[4] When any degree of intimacy between two males (or two females for that matter) is viewed with such suspicion, what do we do when we want to talk to each other about something in a deeper way?

Often it's the case that we men talk to women; that way we feel much more comfortable. This can be a good thing, but you do have to be careful. These situations can quickly become confusing and difficult, and so both parties need to exercise some self-awareness. It's easy to mistake the feeling of 'I can talk to this person, they understand me' with the feeling of 'Wow, at last, someone who understands. I want to marry this person!' – or at least snog them. On the other hand, the person being confided in can easily misconstrue the interest that you are showing them. They can, not unreasonably, think that as you are telling them things that you would not tell many other people, it's because you are pretty serious about them as a potential partner. Then they are left feeling hurt and confused when your intimate chats have built up your self-confidence high enough for you to go and ask their best friend out! This is all the more painful if you no longer have time for them at all, now that you are happy again. This is a good reason for developing the kind of same-sex friendships that will stand these sorts of chats. It might be slightly less confusing.

Notice that in a situation like the one I've just described, although you've been more open and intimate with one another, in itself the relationship isn't friendship. There's more to it than that, which brings us neatly back to the things that you listed when you were advertising for a friend. What were those qualities again?

Well, obviously I don't know what you've written, but I suspect that these are a few of the things that feature on most of our lists. We want our friends to be loyal and trustworthy. We want them to be interested in us for who we are, not for what we do or don't have. More than that, we want them to appreciate us. We want them to have time for us. We would like them to listen to our deepest secrets without laughing at us and telling all their friends. It would help if they have similar interests to ours and if they like the same music and laugh at the same things that we do. We aren't too interested in people who will sit in judgment over us all the time, but maybe they'd be prepared to tell us gently the odd uncomfortable truth every now and again, because that's what honest friendship is all about. We'd like them to be asking about us and interested in the answers. We would like someone to stand by us when others don't, even if this might make them unpopular. We want to be friends with someone who wants the best for us. Someone who will both laugh and cry with us if necessary. And we reserve the right to add to this list if we want to! (In all the times I've done this exercise with groups of people, it's interesting to see that never once has anyone said that their friend has to be good-looking – which is most comforting to those of us who are cosmetically challenged!)

It's quite a list, isn't it? We're obviously not looking for very much from our friends, are we! With expectations within a relationship being so high, you can see why we've been talking about experiencing true and deep friendship only with one or two people at best. Most of us will be fortunate to receive that degree of friendship from one person in our life.

Now, no prizes for guessing that there's a catch here too. Go back to that list of qualities and characteristics. How many of them do you fulfil yourself? Could you honestly answer the advert that you've written? I dare say there are weaknesses that jump out at you. Maybe, like me, you're aware that you don't take the interest in other people that you might. I know a few people who are great examples that really stand out as being interested in other people from the questions that they ask in conversation. The next time you meet them, they remember what you told them and ask how the situation has developed. Guard friends like that! They aren't that interested in settling for superficial chit-chat, and in return are open about the joys and the struggles they're going through. I'm fortunate enough to know a few people like that and they aren't completely earnest either – they're tremendous fun to be with. If I'm not careful I find that I can spend half the night with them talking about my life rather than finding out how they are doing. They are a warning to me as well as an inspiration. I need to be more interested in other people. What stands out for you in the list you wrote as something you could become better at?

Whatever it is, if you realize that you're not actually up to the standard you should be, then maybe it's time to work on being a better friend to someone. And I mean *someone*, not everyone. If we were able to supply that kind of friendship to everyone we met, we'd be very popular for a while and would certainly attract a lot of visitors to our hospital-bed when the collapse came. We just couldn't do it, could we? As it is, it can be hard enough to find the time to see all the people that we want to. This is particularly difficult for people just starting out on their careers. While not all of us have jobs to go to, those who do have one commonly find that they are expected to work longer and longer hours. Often, when they get home, the last thing they then feel like doing is investing the time and effort into building friendships. 'Vegging out' in front of the box with a meal for one seems like a lot less hassle. If you have two couples in that situation (meals for two being the only difference) things become even worse, particularly if they have church commitments and want to play sport or do an evening class too. How do you find the time in four people's diaries to get those two couples together for a drink and a pizza? I wish I had a secret formula to solve that sort of problem. I don't. What this does show, however, is how important it is to make some difficult decisions about where to spend time and who we spend it with.

Hold on, though. Isn't this supposed to be all about having better friendships? Well, I think the key thing in having better friendships is to *be* a better friend. It won't guarantee success, because it's obviously possible to be a lot of things on the list to someone and then for them continually to throw it all back in your face. If that's the case, maybe it's about time you found another friend. But being a better friend yourself sets a great foundation for a deep friendship with someone.

This business of being the best friend that you can be to a best friend is not the easiest thing in the world to do. Perhaps even unconsciously we tend to think about our friendships in terms of what we can get out of them rather than what we can give to them. We'd all much rather have people being to us all the things on our list than for us to go through the hard work of doing and being those things for the benefit of someone else. But this is exactly the sort of instruction that the first Christians were given in working out their relationships,[5] and it's timeless advice that still stands up today. We'll see this in more detail when we look at the kind of love that Christians should demonstrate in their boy/girl relationships. The principles of selfless love that I outline in 'Let's stick together', the chapter about marriage, in fact apply to all of our relationships.

On the face of it some of this might seem really bizarre. A lot of the ideas we've been looking at are completely counter-cultural; they aren't accepted wisdom in the eyes of most people today. It all seems a bit idealistic too, doesn't it? When we're talking about being part of a generation that is on its guard, because we've been hurt before, it is not easy to make ourselves vulnerable and allow people to get close enough, possibly only to hurt us again. The potential for it to happen all over again is there. But what's the alternative?

It hardly bears thinking about. The alternative is a life spent retreating into a sub-human world of isolation and superficiality, never allowing yourself to feel a deep affinity with another person. It's a life spent nursing scars, a life of fear and probably bitterness too. Well, if you're a Christian you are actually *commanded* to live in a different way! And when you see the consequences of *not* trying to work things out in the way that Jesus teaches, you see the reason for those commands. Jesus doesn't teach these things because he wants us to get hurt again, but because only by dealing with issues and working them out can we move forward again. That way we can develop friendships and in the process grow as people. Jesus wants the best for us.

As a result we should be able to work at being a good friend to someone else, and this is equally true whether we are looking at a platonic or a sexual relationship. All that we have looked at so far will be equally relevant to either type of relationship.

What I want to do now, though, is to look particularly at the issues relevant to a sexual relationship between a man and a woman. When we say that Jesus wants the best for us, this applies to our sexual relationships too.

Perhaps the most commonly asked question at this point is: If this is the case, how do I know who I should go out with? How do I work out who I should spend the rest of my life with? (Perhaps we'd also do well to consider whether we should get married at all!) These are the 'small' questions that we're going to consider in the next chapter!

4. is she really going out with him?
guidance

Now Moses ... led the flock to the far side of the
desert and came to Horeb, the mountain of God.
There the angel of the LORD appeared to him in
flames of fire from within a bush. Moses saw that
though the bush was on fire it did not burn up. So
Moses thought, 'I will go over and see this strange
sight – why the bush does not burn up.'

When the LORD saw that he had gone over to look,
God called to him from within the bush,
'Moses! Moses![1]

It was all right for Moses. If we heard God speak out of
a burning bush, I think even the most hard of hearing
amongst us would sit up and pay attention. Not for him
the hours of agonizing about what he should do with
his life; God intervenes in a most dramatic way and
Moses knows emphatically what he should do. He's
been chosen to lead God's people out of exile. Even then
he doesn't like it much though, and tries his best to
wriggle out of it!

Why doesn't God speak to you like that as *you* look for
guidance? Wouldn't it be so much easier to work out
what you should do with your life if you were spoken to
in a way that you couldn't ignore? The whole issue of
guidance is a vexing one for many people, and I reckon

that near the top of the list of things about which we look for guidance is 'Who should I go out with?' Or, even bigger, 'Who should I spend the rest of my life with?'

Well, we don't see too many burning bushes these days. I have no doubt that God is still quite capable of guiding us in such ways and that there are times when he does. But such experiences are very much the exceptions rather than the norm. There is a lot that we can say about the kind of guidance that God gives us though, so before we get into the issue of choosing our life-long partners, it would be helpful to look at some general principles of guidance.

We ask for guidance for all manner of things, not just who we should go out with. We might pray to God for help before a driving test or exam, or want guidance about the kind of job we'll have, and which town or even country we should live in. To ask for guidance is a healthy thing. It's a recognition that we have decisions to make, some of which are pretty far-reaching. It also acknowledges, tacitly, that we don't know everything and that we need some help from somewhere. Or maybe it's a sudden realization that we are in deep trouble and can't get out of it ourselves. Whatever the reason for our requests, the fact that we often seek supernatural help from God at these times is also a recognition, however vague, that we want some help from a higher power. This is the case when we pray to God.

In asking God for guidance, we assume that he can and will give it to us, even if, like Moses, we then decide we don't fancy it very much and go on to question it. That's a correct assumption to make, because one of the attributes that the Bible gives to God is that of Guide.[2] There'd be no point in asking God for guidance about something if he wasn't in the business of giving it. Other images that are used to describe God, such as the Good Shepherd,[3] our Counsellor[4] and, classically, our Father,[5] reinforce this idea. This is instructive too, as the way we are guided, and the kind of guidance that we can expect, are shaped by our understanding of God. If we regard God as uninterested in our day-to-day life and perhaps at best in the distance somewhere when we're in a church building, then we won't expect to hear much from him. In fact we may not even consider it worth asking him for guidance in the first place.

Perhaps we have a choice of suitors, or five proposals of marriage to consider (which is the sort of thing that I'm sure happens to all of us on a regular basis!). Our view of God will shape what we think we hear from him. If, for instance, we visualize God as watching us, waiting to jump on every mistake and making sure that we don't have any fun with our lives, then we'll be looking for those qualities in the guidance we expect from him. We are more likely, as a result, to *distrust* our feelings[6] if we think that God seems to be saying that we should be pursuing our favourite option. Surely God wouldn't want me to be *that* happy; wouldn't it be more character-building for me to marry someone lower down my list? No pain, no gain – and all that perseverance would be so good for me!

Let's take an equally absurd example from the opposite end of the spectrum. Because we think that God wants the best for us, we may therefore assume that this means he'll give us *whatever* we want. We're in for a shock then if we think he is guiding us to marry number three on the list, even though we may spend the whole of our time arguing with gorgeous number two and number one is married anyway. More shocking still, perhaps marrying any of them is a bad idea.

If our sense of guidance is inevitably guided by what we know about God, then it is important that we know God well. And if, as the Bible claims, God's character is unchanging, the best place we can go to ensure that our view of him is accurate is back to the Bible. There are many passages that reaffirm that God knows and cares about us passionately as individual people – both for you and for me.[7] Whether we like it, or can handle it, or not. Whether we like him or not.

Go back to those titles that we found in the Bible which describe God (Guide, Shepherd, Counsellor, Father), and ask yourself, 'What do they tell me about him?' For instance, the fact that it is possible for God to be addressed, even by you and me, as 'Father' should be quite a good start.

We all have differing experiences of what 'father' means. Some of us have never known one. Others will have known their fathers but will not associate them in any way with the attributes of God. So we need to qualify what Jesus means when he talks of God as 'Father'. The way that Jesus talks about our Father gives us plenty to go on. Here is a father who wants to give his children good things, who won't give them a snake as a cruel practical joke when they have asked him for bread.[8] What loving father would? And our daily bread is the first thing we are told to ask for from our Father. So God is the kind of father who won't give us something horrible when we've asked for something good.

Neither will God give us something that is bad for us if we ask for it. He isn't going to give us a snake just because we've asked for it. He knows that, while we might think it's a good idea, it isn't going to do us any good to have one. At the moment, my daughter is just beginning to toddle around and pull herself up on to the furniture. She has quickly developed a fascination for the mugs of tea that I rest on the arm of my chair. She sees me enjoying a drink and decides that it looks so much fun that she'd like to join in. She doesn't understand yet how hot the drink is, and that she'd be hurt if I let her take a mouthful. I have to correct my daughter when she lunges across and makes a grab for the mug, because it would do her no good at all to get what she wants. No good father would fail to warn their children that they are in danger of getting hurt. God doesn't want to see us hurt any more than we do. Sometimes we make the mistake of thinking that, because God wants the best for us, he will give us what we want, when we want it. Actually, because he's a loving father who doesn't want a bunch of spoilt children running around, he won't necessarily give us the car/job/holiday/computer/house/lottery jackpot/person that we want. If we are looking to follow Jesus, we shouldn't expect it to make us rich in terms of material things. Neither should we be seeing people in terms of ownership.

The picture here, then, is of a father who enjoys giving good things to his child. What kind of guidance will you expect to receive from such a father? Well, for a start, you can assume that it will be *good*. It won't lead you up a blind alley for no reason; and because God wants to give you good things, he will not want you to have to play hide and seek in order to find this guidance. That's not to say that working things out will always be a cinch, as life is usually a complicated affair. But God won't be hiding his guidance in order to mock you for not already knowing what to do. He's not that kind of father!

Having established that God wants to guide us and wants the best for us, how does he actually give us guidance? There are a number of ways that God reveals things to us, but the chief one must be through the Bible. It is through the Bible that Christians believe God has revealed himself to us – both his character and his nature. If God is by nature unchanging, and if he has revealed so much about himself and about what he wants for us through the words that we find in the Bible, then it stands to reason that we aren't going to be guided to do something that contradicts the Bible.

Here's an obvious example. You might feel very strongly attracted to someone and decide that it would be great to be married to that person. If either you or the other person are already married, then however strongly you may feel that you are being led to settle down together, you can be absolutely sure that the strong feeling that you have is your own. God cannot be guiding you through this feeling for a married person because it contradicts what we already know about God. The Bible shows us that God has an exceptionally high view of marriage, as we'll see in the next chapter.

That God doesn't contradict himself may seem painfully obvious, but in the passion of falling for someone it's easy to start justifying intense feelings. Feelings can't always be trusted, however tempting it might be to believe that the way you feel is divinely ordained. It isn't unheard of for someone to use 'feeling led' to justify being married for a fourth time when equally they had been 'guided' to marry spouse numbers two and three as well. Does God guide us to be married for a while and then to divorce for another person? No, of course not.

So, if the Bible is so important to the whole process of guidance and we're trying to work out who we are to go out with or to marry, what does it say to help us? Well, we clearly need to use the Bible sensibly and responsibly, engaging our God-given brains as we do so. Otherwise we end up opening it at random and asking for a sign. If we do this, then women with biblical names such as Ruth and Esther will get asked out a lot, while Alisons and Michelas are in for a less busy time on the relationships front! What are the guidelines that the

Bible sets out for us as Christians if we are looking for a partner?

Actually, there are only a few guidelines and they are fairly basic. First, when we're looking for someone to marry, we need to look for someone of the opposite sex. Nowhere in the Bible is it advocated that marriage should be anything other than a man and a woman becoming one flesh.[9] Secondly, the many warnings that the Bible contains concerning adultery tell us that both yourself and your intended must be unmarried.[10] Thirdly, in the light of what Jesus teaches about the grounds for divorce, there may be some divorced men and women who are excluded from your choice too.[11] In addition, we are excluded from marrying certain people because we are too closely related to them or because they aren't of the legal age to marry. Fifthly, and finally, if we are Christians looking for a life-long partner, then that partner needs to be a Christian as well. This is the guideline that often causes the most heartache and problems for people, so let's take a quick look at where we get it from.

Corinth, a city close to two harbours and an important trade centre, was notorious for its sexual (mis)behaviour. Legend has it that there were a thousand temple prostitutes in the city, and Plato used the euphemism 'Corinthian girl' for 'prostitute'. Indeed, 'to act like a Corinthian' was a term used to describe sex outside of marriage. It's against this background that Paul writes his letters to the church there, and it's not surprising that people who had recently turned to follow Jesus had problems adapting to a new way of life and a new lifestyle.

No wonder then that Paul devotes so much time to talking about sex and marriage in his letters to the Corinthians. One of the guidelines that he gives to the church is that widows are free to remarry if they want to (though Paul clearly thinks that they are better off staying single if they can).[12] The only stipulation that he makes is that a widow is to marry another Christian: 'he must belong to the Lord'. This is unlikely to be an instruction exclusive to widows, and we see this idea supported in Paul's second letter to Corinth when he warns Christians, 'Do not be yoked together with un-believers'.[13]

The picture of being yoked together is that of a pair of oxen harnessed together and working in the fields. A modern equivalent might be of two people tied together in a three-legged race. If you are yoked together, you have to work as a team if you are going to get anywhere. It's no good if you are trying to head off in different directions. This warning isn't exclusively about Christians marrying people who don't share their commitment to the faith, but it's difficult to imagine how two people could be more closely yoked than in the intimacy and commitment that should be present in a marriage relationship. Not being unequally yoked means that it's extremely unwise to marry someone who isn't a Christian, or even go out with them for that matter.

That might seem very restrictive to you. There's all

this available talent around and so little of it goes any-where near a church. But you probably don't have to think about it very much to realize that it makes a great deal of sense. Living the Christian life is counter-cultural. We are called to redefine our attitudes to everything: the way that we handle our money, our time, our sexuality. It has implications for our work and family life, and ultimately means acknowledging that we are no longer in charge. There's a new rule to live under; Jesus is in charge now. This makes no sense at all to anyone who hasn't made a commitment to Christ. Such a partner might be most understanding and toler-ate your strange ways, but if it truly made sense to them they would join you and make a commitment too. With the challenge of following Jesus being such a radical one, affecting every area of our lives, you can't expect that you and your partner will both be pulling in the same direction.

It's by no means unknown, but outside of the Christian faith it's an unusual person who believes that sex should be reserved exclusively for marriage. If you're going out with someone, and presumably feel a great deal for them, the sexual side of your relationship is extremely likely to become something of a battle-ground. We know full well that this is the case when two Christians are in a relationship, and we'll go on to look at that in more depth later. But if you are in a rela-tionship with someone who doesn't share your views on sex outside marriage, the battle is much harder. For a start, only one of you is fighting it. If you're in that sort of situation, whose standards will come out on top? The temptation will be either to compromise or to give in altogether.

You may well have the very best intentions about helping the person you are going out with to become a Christian, and sometimes that happens. More often, though, I've known people make a fleeting commitment, often for fear of losing the person whom they love, or, more commonly, the Christian slips away from their faith. Too many times I've seen people ending up throwing away their faith for the counter-attractions of deciding to live with someone who isn't a Christian. In terms that are uncomfortably stark, I have to ask: which is the most important to you, your relationship with God or your relationship with your boyfriend? Which is the most important to you, your relationship with God or your relationship with your girlfriend? Because, ultimately, that is the kind of extremely painful decision you are having to make.[14]

However lovely your partner is, if they don't share your religious beliefs – which are central to your identity – you can't expect them to see life in the same way that you do. The way that we act is shaped by the way we think and the things that we believe. If those things differ in a couple yoked together, they will spend a great deal of time trying to pull in opposite directions. It's hard enough as it is in relationships, married or not, to work together as a team when both share the same outlook, goals and beliefs. In a partnership between a committed Christian and someone who doesn't believe, there will be a great deal of tension and frustration. Sometimes overlooked is the difficulty that the person who doesn't believe will have. Often people in this position will struggle with feeling inadequate because they don't seem able to share in an area of life that is so important to their partner. Others feel angry or suspicious about their partner going off to church every five minutes, and the friendships that they have there. Some feel pressurized into becoming a Christian and get fed up with being insensitively told by well-meaning people how dreadful they are. Others understandably don't want their hard-earned cash going to something that they see as providing a crutch for weak people, and then they worry that their partner needs a crutch. Do you see just some of the areas of conflict that arise from being 'unequally yoked'? The prohibition that the Bible gives is not because God is malicious and wants to narrow down the field. It is there because we are incredibly precious to him, and our relationship with him has been restored at great cost. Astonishingly, God wants the best for us and he doesn't want to lose us.

So, if we are thinking about getting married, there are these five guidelines to help us choose. At first it might seem a little like starting a diet; you look at the list of foods that you aren't allowed and wonder what on earth is left to eat. Actually, it doesn't take a lot of looking at that list to realize that there are a lot of people that you could marry, even if you follow the guidelines. This range of choices is one of the reasons we seek guidance in the first place to know who to go out with or who to marry. If we were living in a culture that denied us this choice and arranged the whole thing for us, we wouldn't have to worry about anything. Well, we'd probably worry a lot actually, about who our parents would choose for a start, but the choice would be out of our hands. As it is we have a freedom of choice, and that includes the freedom, if we are daft enough to choose it, of seeking God's guidance and then ignoring it.

So, we have a choice and God is willing to guide us, as we've already seen from the guidelines that we've uncovered from the Bible. We've also established that he wants the best for us. It's also often said that God has a plan for our lives – so if that plan is the best for me, there must be a person out there who is the one for me; all I need to do is find that person! This is a commonly held view, but I believe that it arises from a misunderstanding of what God's plans for us entail.

The problem with the view that there is one perfect person out there (or, more accurately, that there is a person out there who is perfect for you) is this: it assumes that God has a detailed blueprint for each of our lives. It assumes that he has a perfect will for each of us for every aspect of our lives – not just for whom we should marry or what job we should try to get. It implies that we therefore have to work out what each step of the way should be and try not to depart from that plan at any stage – otherwise we would be outside of God's perfect plan for us. Taken to a stupid extreme, however, this means that we would need to spend time in prayer waiting to be guided about what we should eat for breakfast, for example. In fairness, I don't think anyone in their right mind would advocate this! It stands to reason that the perfect plan is less detailed than this.

I would argue that the plan is a great deal broader. God does have a perfect plan for the way that I live my life. He doesn't want me to live a life that is independent of him. The fact that Jesus died a painful and bloody death on a cross in order to re-establish a relationship with us is all the evidence we need for this. God wants us to live in relationship with him and to become more and more like Jesus. This has implications for the way that we work and the way we relate to all manner of people. God wants us to serve him in all that we do, to live out our faith wherever we are and whoever we are with. I believe that this is God's perfect plan for us. To live with him, for him, and by the commandments he gives us. The rest are details. Sometimes God will intervene, dramatically or not, and make it clear what he wants you to do. At other times it doesn't seem to bother him too much whether you become a tax official or a traffic warden (and astonishingly God loves both!). Ultimately the job that we do in life is far less important than the attitude with which we work and who we are serving in that work. Similarly, within the guidelines that we've already outlined, we might have a relationship with Jo(e) or Chris. There's a choice to be made. It is ultimately less important who you have a relationship with than *how* you conduct that relationship. This is the plan as it is outlined in the Bible.

That isn't to say that you should go out either with

Jo(e) or with Chris though. The fact that you have two people to choose between doesn't mean that you should choose either: they might both be disastrous for you! If you're in a position to make that kind of decision and don't seem to be hearing God speak one way or the other, you have to start employing your God-given grey matter. There are some obvious and basic questions to ask of God and yourself in trying to decide. Questions such as do we like each other, do we have anything in common, could I see myself having a spiritual and emotional relationship with this person, or do I simply fancy this person something rotten? If it's serious, how do they see their future? If I can see myself going to live and work among the people of Africa or Cleethorpes in the future, how does the other person feel about it? Are they as committed to wanting to see some spiritual growth in their life as I am in mine? These are important considerations in choosing a partner for life. Do consider them.

It isn't enough for a man (it's usually the bloke) to go up to a woman and tell her that God has told him that they are going to get married. Imagine how difficult this makes it for the woman to say that she doesn't feel the same way; the refusal seems tantamount to rejecting God's will. I once heard about a woman who thought that she heard God say that a certain man, who she wasn't going out with, would be her husband. She was a wise woman, so she didn't tell him, perhaps in part because the idea filled her with horror! They've been married a long time now. Some people have a distinct feeling from God that they should marry one another. It's happened that way for them, and they do get married. But I've met far more people who have said that they are going out with each other because they have heard it's right from God only to see them split up, sometimes after only a few weeks. The point is that we might hear from God, but we are hard of hearing. We aren't naturally in tune with God, and quite frankly we often use God to legitimate our feelings for someone. So we'll talk about 'feeling led' to go out with someone, which might well be the case, as it might indeed be God who leads us. More often it simply seems to be the case that we want to go out with someone we really like. And if it's the latter, then that's no bad motive in itself, we are free to make that choice. After all, there are worse reasons for going out with someone than that they fit the criteria that we mentioned earlier and that we like them. In fact, that strikes me as a pretty useful start for deciding that you'll go out together.

As the sole criteria for getting married, however, it's rubbish! Feeling or having a hunch that something is 'right' isn't enough. Feeling good about something isn't enough for making such an important decision. If we're feeling good about someone we're happy, and every song on the radio means something. We ourselves aren't necessarily going to be the best objective judges of the situation. This is particularly the case if someone has asked you to marry them. If that happens, the chances are that your emotions are all over the place.

In the midst of all the excitement we can easily get

carried away and lose track of some basic commonsense rules. Marriage is a big step, and hopefully a decision that you're only ever going to make once. That being the case, it is sensible to make sure that you get to know the other person as well as possible. This means spending time together, which isn't usually a problem to couples who are fairly keen on each other. In fact the opposite is often the case, as we pointed out earlier; you might well need to work at spending some time apart every now and again. You need to find out how well you get on together. Do you like the same things, are you able to talk and pray about what's going on in your life together, do you have similar outlooks on life? Do you both want to get married?

It would also be worth your while to talk to some people who know you well and who you can trust to be honest (and sensitive too). They have the advantage of knowing you, and perhaps your intended too, and yet they are able to take a step back and see an angle of the relationship that you may not be able to. You'll have to ask them. They are unlikely to come and tell you if they think you're making a terrible mistake; they are well aware that such advice is rarely welcomed.

This whole idea of the compatibility of a couple was at one time a big issue in terms of the couple's sex life. The theory is still quite popular that it makes sense to sleep with your partner, and maybe other people too, in order to establish that you were 'sexually compatible', whatever that might mean. I should have thought that it was a matter of some pretty basic biology, but that's another matter. The strange thing is that the very best way to work out whether you are compatible as people is not to have sex. That's right, I said *not* to. It's often the case when a relationship starts to become sexual, that sex becomes the main focus of the relationship. Suddenly there's a lot less communication, because there are all these exciting physical things going on. Rather than getting to know someone better, sex can actually act as a barrier to just that.

That sounds dreadfully old-fashioned, doesn't it? For most people, to hear talk of not having sex before marriage sounds hugely idealistic. It's the stuff of fairy tales and bad romance novels. But it's exactly the position that the Bible outlines, and with good reason, as we're about to see.

5. everyone else is doing it so why can't we?
the Bible and sex

'What's this idea of sex, sex, sex all the time?
In the old days one didn't know about it at all. I'd had
six or more proposals of marriage before I knew
how babies came. Nobody talked about it, and I think
it was better.' *Barbara Cartland*

It feels deeply uncomfortable to stand alone against popular opinion. It's hard work swimming against the tide, to be saying and doing things that mark you out as different. Most of us want to blend in and be like other people. Peer pressure – the pressure to be like our friends – is massive.

We're very aware of peer pressure amongst children in school and during the teenage years, but seem to be blind to it when we're older and yet still victims of it. There's a pressure to conform to the ethic of the workplace, in working long hours or fiddling your expense form. The language you use can easily change according to the people that you are among; the way you behave on the sports field might well be different to the way you are in church. Deep down we all want to be popular, and so we shy away from doing or saying things that mark us out, especially if we fear that being different might be something that's scorned. We don't like to be uncomfortable. We hate to be ridiculed.

We also live in a culture which seems to be obsessed with sex. Women's magazines have long been offering advice on things like 'Secrets of your sexuality', 'What makes a woman good in bed?', and 'Hot sex! – Answer 20 questions and it's yours'.[1] More recently, there have been a bunch of new titles aimed at men which address sex from a male perspective: 'Men behaving badly – Sleeping around after the big break up', 'Do British men make better lovers?' and 'The naked truth – what women want from your body'.[2] In addition to this, 'experts' in the field, such as TV's Dr Ruth, assert that 'sexual pleasure is your natural right'.[3]

The reason that these things are being advertised on the covers of magazines is because publishers know we want to read them, and sex sells issues – particularly if the article can play on our insecurities about how we rate in bed and promise us better sex and an improved performance. Tabloids would have us believe that the sex stories they peddle are big news which are reported in the public interest. (We may well be interested, but that's very different to it being in our interests to know.) What is really going on is thinly veiled titillation. It sells. The same goes for much of the stuff we see on video or on the TV. How much of what we see is there because it's crucial, or even vaguely important to the plot? We could add to that the question, How realistic is much of what we see and read about? In these accounts sex is usually fulfilling, ecstatic and clichéd. It's never ever messy or difficult. And, of course, that makes it all the easier to sell magazines to you next time around! We seem to be surrounded by people having great sex. We know that they're having great sex because they then go and write songs about it which we hear on the radio, they tell reporters who print it in newspapers, or they act it out on video. Closer to home they're talking about it in the canteen, the office or the bar.

If you aren't having sex, you're seen as being a bit strange by a lot of the people around you. They would echo the view of Oscar Wilde that celibacy is 'the only known sexual perversion'. For most people sex has become just another part of going out with someone. This is reflected in the fact that, by 1994, only 1% of men and 4% of women in the UK were still virgins when they got married.[4]

Add together wanting to be like your mates and the fact that we are living in a culture where everyone else appears to be enjoying a great sex life. Christians who try to stand out and be different in the way they behave in relationships are under enormous pressures. Everybody else is doing it, so why can't we? This is a big temptation for a lot of people, especially at college or at the office Christmas party where getting off with someone is relatively easy. Alcohol is cheap or even free, and you're surrounded by lots of attractive people. Not only that but they become more attractive with every drink! Once you've fled the family nest and there aren't the restrictions of parents knowing when you get in (or if), you have a great deal of freedom. How will you use that? Do you go with the flow? The great temptation is

to do just that. Why resist it? Unless you have a positive set of principles for not getting involved, the
chances are that you will give in.

In researching this book, I conducted a survey among
a number of people between the ages of 18 and 22. The
survey was completed by 140 students in Christian
Union meetings, all of whom identified themselves as
being Christians.[5] When they were asked what the
Bible teaches about sex and relationships, many had to
confess that they didn't really know.[6] It's not entirely
their fault. No-one has told them. Even many of those
who had heard talks about the subject betrayed their
lack of teaching from the way that they answered other
questions. We can't follow the teaching of the Bible on
the way we should conduct ourselves sexually if we
don't really know what it says on the topic. We end up
taking our cue from our culture instead, and that can be
disastrous.

One of the great things about the Bible is that it does
talk to us about sex. We may not always appreciate
what it has to say, but it does nevertheless give us valuable guidelines for enjoying sex. (Yes, that's right, I said
enjoying sex.) Let's go back to the beginning of the Bible
and see where we get this whole idea about marriage
from in the first place.

We saw earlier on, right at the beginning of the
Bible, that men and women were created by God in his
image, both male and female.[7] Although 'marriage'
isn't specifically mentioned, Genesis 2:24 outlines what
is clearly to become the norm for those who marry: 'a

man will leave his father and mother and be united to his wife, and they will become one flesh.' This verse, which both Jesus and Paul quote,[8] outlines what we expect to find in marriage. It is a public act, implied by the man leaving his mother and father, and it involves a commitment to another person for life: they become one flesh. Implied too is that this public act is a 'covenant relationship'; that is; that both parties give and receive promises to one another. They promise each other that they are free to leave ('no lawful impediments') and prepared to cleave ('I do'). Marriage is established then as the setting for the closest one-flesh relationship between a man and a woman.

Other teaching in the Bible supports this. There are a great number of warnings against breaking this one-flesh covenant and committing adultery. The one prohibition on adultery that most people remember from the Bible is the seventh of the ten commandments that God gave to Moses.[9] Yet there are just as many warnings, many of them frighteningly stark, in the New Testament about committing adultery. Jesus has plenty to say on the subject.

Indeed, he seems to raise the stakes significantly when, in the course of his teaching, he discusses adultery.[10] Jesus points out that his followers should know that it's wrong to commit adultery, because they are told so in the commandments given to Moses. But then he says that even to look at someone lustfully is effectively to commit adultery with them in your heart. There can't be too many of us who can read those words and can honestly say that we aren't guilty of looking lustfully at someone else. Jesus' words are a challenge to us and the way we live each day. Jesus warns us here not to fantasize about people. These words also cut to the heart of the struggle that so many of us have about whether it is acceptable for Christians to use pornography or to masturbate. This has implications for the thoughts we entertain and for the things we watch on TV or video. Jesus sets us a very high standard here, and there can't be many of us who can honestly say that we haven't got it wrong in one of these areas. Surveys show that these are the things that people struggle with most.[11]

It's clear that in the teaching that prohibits adultery, and warns against even thinking about it, marriage is protected and held up as something extremely valuable. Those vows to love one another 'till death do us part' are serious ones. They are a promise of fidelity. We aren't to risk the marriage for the sake of sex with someone else, however attractive or comforting that might seem at the time. We don't promise to stay together until we fancy a change or a more attractive option presents itself. These are big vows. They aren't promises to be made without serious thought.

A further indication of the high value that God attaches to marriage is underlined by Malachi 2:16 where he says that he hates divorce. That's pretty unequivocal; there isn't a lot of margin for misunderstanding here! And yet, perhaps surprisingly, divorce is permitted in certain circumstances. As Jesus continues to teach, having just warned his followers about adultery, he then restates the importance of marriage in teaching about divorce. The law of the Old Testament said that a man could write a certificate and present it to his wife if he found 'something indecent about her'.[12] Referring to this, Jesus tightens up the divorce laws considerably by saying that divorce is only permissible in cases of marital unfaithfulness. If someone in a marriage commits adultery, then divorce is an option. In addition to this, Paul writes to the Corinthian church that if you are a Christian married to someone who doesn't believe and that person wants to leave, you should let them go.[13] These, though, are very much the exceptions. Marriage is very highly regarded throughout the Bible, and a part of the vow that is made in a Christian marriage is that sex is to be confined to that marriage. This isn't just because marriage is so highly prized but also because sex is regarded as such a precious gift, given by God to his people. It's too precious to be enjoyed outside the intimate relationship of marriage. For their own good, men and women who are married are not free to have sex with whoever they please, whenever they please.

You have only to see the pain and devastation that adultery causes to know that these are extremely wise guidelines. The break-up of a marriage due to adultery, or, for that matter, the devastating impact on a marriage where one partner commits adultery and the couple decide to stay together anyway, clearly destroys the lie that is often propagated that adultery can be fun and harmless, and even a safety-valve for a marriage.

It's all very well and good to say that, once you're wed, the sanctity of marriage means you are not to have sex with other people. But my guess is that the vast majority of people who are reading this book will be unmarried. The Bible's view of marriage isn't necessarily the most pressing concern that we have about relationships. What, if anything, does the Bible have to say about sex before marriage?

Well, it won't come as too much of a surprise to learn that the Bible says a great deal. However, we're rather ignorant as to what it does teach on this subject. Most of us find it difficult enough to obey the Bible in any area of our lives. When we're talking about something as deeply personal as our sex lives, it's even harder. We aren't helped when we read something in the Bible and don't have much idea what it means.

In talking to a number of people about this whole issue, I asked them to define for me two terms that Bible translators have used, both of which are key to our understanding of how we are to act sexually if we are unmarried. Have a go at these two terms yourself. They are 'fornication' and 'sexual immorality'. Don't be embarrassed if you struggle with finding definitions for them, about two thirds of the people that I asked couldn't explain them.[14]

Fornication is such an old-fashioned word, isn't it? It's not one in wide usage these days – we might hear it occasionally, but not very often. I read an article in a national newspaper recently which referred to two dogs fornicating, but I can't think when I last heard or read it otherwise. Quite a number of the people I asked thought that fornication was just another word for sexual intercourse, and so, it would seem, did the person who wrote the newspaper article. This has deeply serious consequences, because if this is the definition and there are passages in the Bible warning against fornication, you are unlikely to have a very positive view of sex. But the Bible is actually very positive about sex. For a start there's a whole book, The Song of Songs, which goes on at length about how great sex is. This shouldn't surprise us. After all, God invented it.

People feeling bad about the whole issue of sex are not going to be helped if they think that fornication (and therefore sex) is warned against and that God, at best, allows us to indulge due to our weakness. We might laugh at such an idea, but it's not an attitude that is unknown in church history. Writing nine hundred years ago, Odilon of Cluny was obviously revolted by the thought of sex: 'How can we desire to clasp in our arms the bag of excrement itself?' He clearly knew some great chat-up lines! 'Hey you, you great bag of dung …'

So here's a better definition of fornication, provided by the dictionary: 'voluntary sexual intercourse outside marriage'.[15] It's a far healthier definition in terms of seeing sex in a more positive way, although it will be seen by some as rather old-fashioned in terms of being restrictive. This means that when the Bible warns against fornication, as it does in a number of places, it's saying that you are not to have sex outside marriage, whether you are married or not. That obviously includes sex before marriage.

Let's take a look now at the second of those terms, 'sexual immorality'. This phrase occurs throughout the New Testament, from Jesus to Revelation.[16] But what does 'sexual immorality' mean?

We were saying at the beginning of the book that our generation, labelled X, is one that is suspicious of the big institutions and the big philosophies which seek to explain the whole of life. We don't like to be told by others what our value judgments should be (which might be why you are perhaps irritated by someone writing a book that tells you what the Bible has to say about how you conduct your relationships, for example!). Because of that distrust of people telling us what we should do and think, we like to make up our own minds about things. One of the things that many of us agree on is that there isn't any one way of doing things that works, but different ways to suit us as individuals. You can't say that something is objectively true or false, that something is true for all people everywhere. It therefore becomes the height of arrogance to make an absolute statement. This seems to be especially the case if you want to say, as evangelical Christians do, that there is just the one way to God: Jesus. This is seen as intolerant towards people who have different beliefs. You can say that such a thing is true for you, but that doesn't mean that it has to be true for me. This applies to all manner of things, not just religion, and taken to extremes is shown to be ludicrous.

Consider for a moment the 'truth' that there is no objective truth. This statement poses as an objective and absolute truth, and it is therefore a huge contradiction.

One of the effects of all this is that a lot of us out there are searching for the truth, or at least for a truth. It is, we are told, 'out there'. This means that we are trying to work out our own value systems, and we end up with different ones. So we come across a term like 'sexual immorality' and we are at a bit of a loss to define it, because the things that *you* consider to be sexually immoral *I* might decide are fine. Or vice versa. This confusion is well illustrated by a court case in Britain from the early 1990s when a group of consenting men took it in turns to pierce each other's genitalia using a hammer and nails. The question that taxed judges and journalists was whether what was happening was an offence. If so, what criteria can you use to decide?

So, it would seem, we can disregard the idea of sexual immorality and decide that, so long as we feel comfortable with what we are doing, there is no reason to feel bad or that we are doing anything wrong. This assumes, of course, that we will know what is best for ourselves, that there are no objective standards, and that our consciences are a foolproof method of knowing what is right and what is wrong!

Why then do Bible translators use the term 'sexual immorality'? Good question! Presumably they weren't happy with using 'fornication' because so few people know what this means. Here's the key: both fornication and sexual immorality are ways that the Greek word '*porneia*' has been translated. They both mean the same thing. *Porneia* is a term that covers all extramarital sexual relationships. Thus it is a warning against adultery, prostitutes, homosexuality, sex with animals, and sex before or even instead of marriage. Fornication and sexual immorality are both expressions that refer to sex outside of marriage. Unless it's sex with your husband or your wife, it's off limits; it's sin. This is exactly what we would expect from what we have already seen about the Bible's high view of both marriage and of sex.

So when Paul says sex outside of marriage is wrong, he's talking directly to us and directly challenging the way that we might want to behave. When, for example, Paul is writing to the Galatian church about the things that should mark out Christians, he lists a whole host of characteristics, among them love, patience, faithfulness and self-control. By way of contrast, the first thing that he lists as an opposite form of behaviour is sexual immorality.[17] Here is a vivid reminder to us that, if we are wanting to live as Christians, we are to be different people – different both from those around us and from the way that we've been used to living. We are not to be characterized by sexual immorality. We are to avoid sin. We should be known as people of self-control and patience and faithfulness. We should be people who love in a way that is different, either from the way we used to love or from the way that a lot of people around us love.

It might be that we are well aware of how we've failed

to reach those kinds of standards in the past, and we'll look at this in more detail later. On the other hand, though, it may be that secretly we feel cheated. We take a look around and it seems that everyone else is enjoying themselves while we aren't even supposed to be at the party.

The myth exists, and is actively propagated, that all our peers are having a great time sexually. They're active, and often. It's a sign of their maturity and sophistication that they are able to have sex as part of their relationship, either as part of a committed relationship or as a casual thing between two consenting adults. It's seen too as a sign that they are adults – not for them the immaturity and stigma of virginity. They've grown up! Yet scratch just a little below the surface and you realize that there's a great deal of insecurity and pain behind the façade of so many happy loving couples.

When the survey that I used with students asked whether they regretted anything that they had done sexually, over half said emphatically that they did (54%). Illustrating the confusion that so many feel, another 14% didn't know how they felt, and some of those who said they had no regrets then went on to express them. Just under a third of men and a third of women said that they didn't regret what they had done sexually.

The regrets that people harboured were deeply heartfelt. Able to state their thoughts anonymously, men and women expressed those regrets:

'In the long run, a moment's pleasure isn't worth the pain that follows it.'

'... the sexual sins I committed actually screwed me up in later life ...'

'It may be fun at the time, but afterwards it's hell.'

'Don't kid yourself about what you think you can do ... sleeping in the same bed but not having sex – it's virtually impossible.'

'It's not worth it.'

'I felt cheap and couldn't take back what I'd done.'

'Sex totally changes a relationship, often not for the better.'

'It usually ends in guilt and regret – it's not worth it.'

There's no escaping that a great number of people (the majority, don't forget) have regrets, and that those regrets cause them very real pain.

Ah well, you might want to say, that's all down to the repression that Christians are always putting themselves under. Christians are hung up about sex, inside and outside marriage. No wonder they feel all this hurt and regret. Thing is, they aren't alone. A very honest piece of writing in a magazine puts this case very powerfully from the perspective of a woman who notices what has happened to her as a result of having a large number of relationships.

'I've thrown beer and strops in equal quantities, had my share of sobbing in toilets and on friends' sodden shoulders – and a result of all this: I have developed an icy stare that can pierce skin, a sarcastic tone that can strip flesh, and enough cynicism to make a nasty mess of what's left.' The author then goes on to describe a situation where she felt great rejection at meeting a friend who, less than twelve hours earlier, had left her bed. They were meeting mutual friends and she recalls '... the look of panic on his face when I walked over to him. He thought I might show that we'd been together.'[18]

Sex with a series of partners feels unsatisfying and results in developing a protective shield of cynicism. The thinking is that you are less likely to get hurt through a casual sexual relationship because you've engaged with one another in a slightly detached way. You've been holding back something of yourself and treated this as a fairly casual thing: you may see the other person again, it may lead to something more, but no-one's thinking much beyond the moment for now.

The only problem with this approach is that it doesn't work! Lots of us can identify with the point made by the writer of the magazine article that, however casual a fling might seem to be, you can't just switch off and observe the moment. Sex isn't like that. There's a well-established myth that you can have safe sex: if you use a condom, the chances of unwanted children and/or catching something horrible are greatly reduced. But that's as far as it goes. It's impossible to have protected sex – sex that is entirely risk-free and safe – because sex isn't just a genital encounter. It's so much more than that, and until someone comes up with a condom for the heart, there can never be safe sex. (And who wants a condom for the heart anyway, reducing sex to the level of a genital encounter? Give me the erotic over the robotic anytime.)

Sex involves being incredibly vulnerable with someone. Naked with someone, there isn't a lot of room for pretence. Here you are, you're offering yourself to someone else, you're taking a risk. What if they take one look and laugh? Having been that vulnerable with a person, the sense of rejection and sometimes the sense of having been used, when they no longer return your phone calls, is debilitating. Sex can be immensely satisfying but it can never be safe. And it's because it isn't safe that God says sex should be confined to marriage.

We might feel a little cheated that all our friends, those who seem so sophisticated and grown up, are having sex, while God is saying throughout the Bible that we are not to. It all seems so unfair, not to mention old-fashioned. But God doesn't command this because he's some kind of killjoy who wants us to suffer and keep repressive rules for the sake of it. He tells us to obey these instructions because they are good for us. Having invented it, he knows how sex works best: in a loving, committed relationship. The safest place to enjoy that level of intimacy is within marriage where there is the highest level of commitment pledged to one another. It's a far safer environment for true intimacy than any other arrangement, including cohabitation. We'll argue about that one later on in the chapter 'Let's stick together'.

Far from being repressive, as these rules might seem, they are in fact enormously freeing. If we were to live by them, we'd be freed from the emotional damage that so many of us feel after having had a series of failed sexual relationships. We'd be free to enjoy a sexual relationship with one life partner, with no secret fears about how we measured up and who we were supposed to be measuring up to. It's a great ideal. Yet the sad truth is that, for lots of us, it's too late. It's already a lost dream. We've already made serious mistakes in the area of our relationships, often greatly regretting them. This is the case whether we've been involved in full sexual intercourse, or stopped short but still regret going as far as we have. The amount of sexual guilt that so many of us feel is crippling. It's time to grab the nettle and be honest about that.

6. like a virgin
we've made some mistakes

'Most people begin sexual intercourse while they are teenagers ... once they begin having sex they nearly always continue, not only with their current partner but afterward with other boyfriends or girlfriends. For most, sex becomes a normal part of dating.'

'According to the Family Research Council's publication *Free to Be Family*, "sexually active 18-year-olds today have had on average more sexual partners than the present group of 40-year-old women has had in their entire lives."' [1]

It's one thing to know what we should be doing; it's quite another thing to be doing it. Having seen what the Bible lays out as the way we should act in our relationships, we know how we should be behaving. Every single one of us is aware, however, that we don't live up to the standards that we have just read about. Even if we've not been in the type of sexual relationship with someone else which the Bible would describe as immoral (*i.e.* sex outside marriage), I doubt that any of us can say that we have not entertained the kind of thoughts that Jesus spoke about. [2]

Not that we're likely to admit that to anyone of course! Sadly, one of the things that is most disturbing about the whole issue of sex and relationships before marriage in Christian circles is the fact that we're so embarrassed by the whole topic that we'd rather not talk about it at all, let alone admit to troubles or temptations. I can't remember hearing a sermon or being part of a Bible study group that dealt with sexuality other than at a very basic level. In that I'm not unusual; some of us have *never* heard a sermon on such a topic at all! That's astonishing when you consider how important it is that we relate properly to each other sexually. More people have been helped by the teaching of a youth group, but a lot of us never went to a youth group, we became Christians later than that. Yet we need to hear what the Bible says on the topic because we aren't likely to ask to hear it. And whether it's in the context of a sermon or in more personal discussion, we're more likely to admit to mass murder than to having any troubles or temptations in the sexual realm.

Yet, perhaps surprisingly, nearly half of the students that I surveyed (47%) had heard Christian teaching on sex-related issues on at least five occasions, mainly in a youth group. This has to be applauded as being a good start when there is such an emphasis on sex on TV and in magazines. It's easy enough to get five unbiblical messages about sex from watching TV for a few hours! We are fed such seductive messages about sex from the media that we need constantly to remind ourselves of God's perspective on things. Sadly, even if we do get the message, we don't always act on it.

Because we find it difficult to discuss these things with other people, many of us feel that we are struggling alone with the way we behave sexually. 'I must clearly be a freak to be suffering in this way, because no-one else seems to be having any problems.' As a result we all battle on alone, worried by the troubles we're experiencing in living up to the Bible's standards, ashamed of the way that we've at times made a mess of things, and feeling terribly isolated. For a start, it would be a help to be able to talk to someone we could trust about all this, perhaps someone older in the church. Most of us don't have this opportunity. The battle to live in a way that honours God in our relationships is a difficult one and one which, if we are honest, we sometimes feel like giving up on altogether. There are times when it all feels too difficult.

Let's start by talking openly here. It won't make pleasant reading, but if we're going to attempt to work this out we won't do it by sweeping the difficult bits under the carpet. The scale of our struggles are far too great to ignore just because we feel uncomfortable talking about them. We won't get anywhere by staying silent because these things are hard to talk about politely.

We need to start by admitting that unmarried Christians are facing great struggles in this area, and there are times when we get it horribly wrong. We aren't sure what we can and cannot do physically within a relationship, and those of us who think we know what our boundary should be are painfully aware that we've broken through that boundary.[3] Most of us, that's right – the majority – have made big mistakes in the area of our sexual relationships. We've done things that we know we shouldn't, we've fallen way below our own standards of behaviour let alone God's, and we feel even worse about ourselves as a result.

Because of the confusion that surrounds what you can or can't do physically when in a relationship with a girl-friend or boyfriend, most of us would feel a great deal happier if someone would set our boundaries for us. How far can we go in our sexual relationships before we're doing something we shouldn't? Most of us are greatly confused by this whole matter of how far we can go. We'd love someone to give us the definitive answer. This is the question that vexes us the most. Guess what? I'm afraid I'm not going to draw that line for you. What I will do, though, is offer you some *guidelines* which will help you decide for yourself.

To start with, we know from what we've learned that sexual immorality is sex outside of marriage, and that God, because he knows what is best for us, has told us not to be in that kind of relationship outside of mar-riage. We therefore know that we aren't to have sex out-side marriage. Let's be honest though, short of full genital intercourse that leaves an awful lot that we could be doing, doesn't it? Where should we stop?

Before looking at that, can I just rephrase the ques-tion in a way that exposes our motives more clearly? We know that we aren't to have sex outside marriage, but we want to know what we *can* do. The questions we are asking are: Can I hold hands / hug / kiss / snog (prolonged kissing)? Is it OK to be petting (caressing my partner with my hands outside their clothing)? How about heavy petting, where I do the same but without or underneath someone's clothes? Then there are the questions of whether mutual masturbation (stimulating my partner's genitals with my hands while they reciprocate) and oral sex (stimulating my partner's genitals by mouth) are acceptable. In summary, how far can we go before what we are doing is wrong? Put bluntly, because this is what we want to know, how much fun can we have before the religion thing kicks in?

Why do we ask that question? We know that as Christians we are trying to follow the teaching of a loving God who wants the very best for us. He wants us to live lives that are the best that they can be. We've already said that the rules that are laid down for sex are there because they make the most sense. They are there for our protection. We decide to play by our own rules at our own peril. If we do, we are very likely to get hurt. If we were being warned about keeping away from a dangerous fire, we'd stay in the safest place, well away from it. It would be perverse to play a game of seeing how close we could get to the fire before we got burned. Yet, no doubt because the fire is so attractive and we'd like a bit of warmth, that's exactly the game that we play with our relationships. And some of us have got scars from the old flames to prove it.

Do you see what I'm getting at here? Instead of trying to stay on safe ground and live out what God tells us is best for us, we try to get away with as much as we can while we (hopefully) retain our virginity. We want to have a foot in both camps. We want to follow God, and we want to be in a position where we are doing the same sorts of things as our mates. We don't want to stand out, and it's not as if we're trying to avoid something that is intrinsically unpleasant. We end up trying to walk a tightrope. In the circumstances it's not surprising that a lot of us end up getting seriously hurt in the process.

We want to adhere to the rules that God has laid down for us, but we are also very attracted to enjoying a sexual relationship. We see it all the time in the media and in the lives of the people around us. So we tend to try to push the boundaries as far as we can and stop just short of full genital intercourse. Not all of us can say that we've succeeded; many of us have fallen off the tightrope altogether. Some of us haven't, but we've come awfully close to it, and we've been left clinging on by our fingertips. Regardless of where we might feel we should draw the boundary, many of us would claim that we are still just about virgins. But, boy, it's been close. We've done virtually everything else on the scale and just managed to stop short of full intercourse. We've stopped at mutual masturbation or oral sex, but we haven't had penetrative sex. We might be virgins but it's really only a technicality. We certainly don't feel particularly virginal.

This business of having as much fun as we can before we have to stop, so as to avoid doing something we shouldn't – it isn't very God honouring, is it? In black and white it doesn't even look particularly convincing, does it? You probably don't need to see the results of a survey to tell you that this is a seriously painful game to play. As we've already seen, so many people have gone beyond the line that they have set themselves, regardless of where they drew that line. And they have deeply regretted it. The moments of pleasure that they experienced haven't turned out to be worth all the time that they've felt awful about what they have done. In addition, many felt bad because they know that they got it wrong as Christians. A lot of us know how that feels, and we carry an enormous baggage of guilt around as a result.

A good number felt even worse because, in addition, they were no longer in that particular relationship any more. Most had been in relationships of intimacy; they hadn't been sexually involved with people merely in a one-night stand. With the break-up in the relationship come extra complications. If you have been sexually intimate with someone who then finishes the relationship, you'll be left with deep feelings of rejection. Many people are also plagued by flashbacks, which all too vividly remind them of what they have done. The feeling of having been used is particularly keenly felt by a lot of women, many of whom feel that there has been a strong degree of pressure from their boyfriends to go further than they feel comfortable with. Of course, it is naïve to assert that all sex before marriage takes place because men seduce women; there are times when the opposite is the case. Whichever side the pressure is coming from, though, there is bound to be tension concerning what you do physically before marriage when there are two opposing viewpoints in a partnership. In the heat of a passionate relationship, such a conflict is unlikely to be resolved by both partners wanting to turn, there and then, to the Bible for guidance. It's vital to have worked out your principles beforehand.

As an example, let's take the case where it is the man who is responsible for most of the pressure to go too far with his girlfriend. After perhaps weeks or months of pressure, however subtle, women often do things that they don't really want to do and regret it. Perhaps they fear losing their boyfriend if they don't. Later, when they break up anyway, the grief that they feel is multiplied. As men we need to understand that this kind of selfishness, however we try to disguise it, isn't doing anyone any favours. Both men and women feel the regret and pain of failing in the way they have behaved sexually. What kind of love are we showing a girlfriend if we are pressuring her into falling short of the standards that we should both be upholding? What kind of love are we showing if we are trying to persuade our partner to sin?[4] As men, are we showing ourselves to be very trustworthy through a situation like this? A friend of mine is about to be married. He and his fiancée are committed to saving sex for marriage. As he pointed out to me, if he doesn't keep his word in this matter before they are married, why should his fiancée trust him when he gives his pledge to remain faithful?

There is a category of people, male and female, who feel the pain of having failed to meet God's standards even more deeply. Often they were determined that they would hold out for the right person, they wanted to wait for Mr or Ms Right. They meet that person and make a pledge to them, probably through getting engaged. Sooner or later that commitment to one another takes the form of greater sexual intimacy, and if you were in the position to raise an eyebrow at their behaviour you'd be told, 'It's OK, we're going to get married.' (Either that or something considerably less polite!) There seems to be a great certainty amongst us that, if we are both committed and engaged, nothing can go wrong. Our feelings and our circumstances won't change, we're on the final lap and approaching the finishing tape, the wedding day itself. It gives me no pleasure to point out that 'it ain't necessarily so'. Too many of us get hurt by that kind of scenario, where one person decides that maybe they are wrong or that they're too young, or they meet someone else, or … fill in the space yourself. Put bluntly, you don't know that you'll actually get married; engagements get broken. If it happens to you, even if you're the one who calls it off, it'll hurt. It will hurt a great deal more if there's a whole load of sexual guilt to work through too.

Even if you make it through and end up getting married and living happily ever after, you're very likely to end up having to work through that sexual guilt, most probably in the early years of marriage. The whole business of pushing the boundaries so that you can have as much 'fun' sexually as possible is a bad idea all round. It hurts us and other people. In addition, there are two other reasons why it's not a very safe game to be playing.

First, and fairly obviously, on the scale that we've mentioned, the space between varying degrees of physical intimacy is by no means equal. Most of us, when we find that we are holding hands with someone that we love, don't become so sexually excited that we feel we need to have sex with that person right away. Most of us can hug someone without wanting there and then to be involved in a prolonged kissing session. Given how much some Christians hug each other, this is an extremely good thing! However, if we are engaged in heavy petting, it is a much shorter step to become involved in mutual masturbation. We've already built up quite a head of steam and are much more sexually excited. Whether we feel what we are doing is a good idea or not, pulling back and stopping is far more difficult than if we wanted to stop holding hands. Someone once described it as having the engine of a Ferrari and the brakes of a bicycle. It's not a bad description.

Wherever we've drawn our line, or if someone was to draw it for us for that matter, our tendency is to push up close to that line. What happens in the vast majority of cases is that we then cross the line. We can redraw it, perhaps in the same place, or, perhaps thinking that our original line was a bit idealistic, we'll move it. But once the line has been crossed, we find it even harder to stick to it. We weren't struck down by lightning, and may well have enjoyed it before we felt so grotty later on, and so we cross the line again. After this has happened a number of times, we either give up trying to draw the line at all or we finish the relationship altogether because we feel so bad about things. Because our brakes are so poor, the wisest and safest thing is not to start the engine in the first place. To avoid getting hurt, be sure to be at a place where it's easy to stop. If you're setting yourself some sort of limit as to how far you're going to go in a relationship because you want to avoid sin in your life, then play it safe and draw the line low. It will help you to avoid a great deal of trouble and hurt later on. One wise saying on the subject is, 'Don't touch anything that you haven't got.' It's good advice.

The second reason for not wanting to play the dangerous game of going as far as you think you can is this: I'm not sure that I know where sex actually begins. Now, as a father, I find that a particularly embarrassing thing to have to admit! Let me try to explain what I mean.

In response to the terrible increase in people becoming infected with the HIV virus and the increased numbers dying of Aids, there has been a big emphasis from Health Authorities on 'safe sex'. Because the HIV virus is often sexually transmitted, there has been a move to reassess sexual activity. Whilst in the past we have tended to think of sex as being the act of penetration, we are now questioning what actually constitutes sex. I believe that this is very helpful to us as we think about the intimacy that is expressed in a physical relationship, because sex is more than the exchange of bodily fluids. Indeed, sex is more than a physical act, and physically it's more than genital intercourse.

As we've already outlined, sex is more than just a grinding of the groins. As well as being a physical act, it is both emotional and spiritual. The fact that it is emotional is well demonstrated by the damage that we feel when we engage in sex inappropriately. This was graphically brought home to me while I was away on holiday. We were in Greece at the end of the holiday season and, as virtually the only ones in a restaurant, got talking to one of the men who worked there. He was very honest and told how he had had hundreds of sexual partners over the past few years. He said how easy it was to pick up girls on holiday, especially if they had seen the film *Shirley Valentine*! He wasn't boasting though, he was deeply regretful of his actions, and repeated several times how wrong what he had done was. Here was a man who was hurting deeply, and his basic problem was that too much casual sex had done him a lot of harm. As he expressed it himself, it had made him a cold and hard character who was dispassionate about sex, it meant nothing to him any more. What should have been a deep and intimate experience had become reduced to the level of, say, eating a meal.

The pain that people feel as a result of playing around with sex is also there because even more goes on within sex than just the physical and the emotional. There's the spiritual element. Sex is a deep bonding between two people; the Bible refers to it as the two becoming 'one flesh'. Paul identifies this as a profound mystery,[5] and is referring to the fact that there is something extraordinarily deep going on during sexual union. The one-flesh union is in the realms of the spiritual as well as the physical and the emotional.

The physical side of sex too, I am sure, is a great deal more than the final item on the list at which we were looking earlier, when we were wondering how far we could go. For a start, sex is a great deal more than the two minutes and fifty-two seconds of squelching that Johnny Rotten described it as. But I have to be honest and admit again that I don't know for sure at what point sex starts. I cannot accept that oral sex (is there a clue in the description there?), for instance, is not a form of having sex. Neither am I convinced that mutual masturbation is not a form of having sex; without doubt it's certainly a sexual act. This confusion about what actually constitutes having sex is another reason that I think many of us have at best a tenuous grip on our virginity. It might even be that we're now no longer sure whether we are virgins or not. When the Bible warns us against sexual immorality – sex outside the context of marriage – I believe we are being warned against these sorts of sexual acts as well as penetrative sex.

With this as a fresh benchmark, we are more deeply aware than ever about the ways we have made a mess of our sex lives. If we were feeling pretty down about things before reading this chapter, we may be positively depressed by now. For many of us our mistakes are branded deep on our consciences, and we know all too well where we've got it wrong. Some of us will know a little guilt but might be less troubled. In the end it makes little difference whether we feel it acutely or not. We are guilty of not living up to the sexual standards that God sets before us. Because we've ignored him in this area of our lives, we've ended up getting hurt. That's hardly surprising now we've learnt that sex is more than the physical; there are deep spiritual and emotional things going on too. We've felt rejection, we've been bitterly disappointed, we've realized that the moments of pleasure were never worth the regrets that lingered on long afterwards. How come it was never portrayed this way in the movies? Sex there is so ecstatic, so much less messy, and always deeply fulfilling. There seems to be so little room for regrets and guilt and worry about whether it was such a good idea after all.

We, on the other hand, away from Hollywood, are left to deal with a job lot of guilt. We are trying to live out our lives as followers of Jesus, and this part of life is just about the hardest thing to cope with. We're feeling strong urges to be active sexually. We have to face up to our failures and the fact that, for many of us, these have been repeated failures. Where do we go from here? Are we locked into this struggle for eternity, or at best until we get married? No – thank God! – we are not.

7. just like
starting over
we can be forgiven

A Gallup poll, reported in *The Times* on 6th July 1996,
shows that less than half of the people questioned
(47%) believe that adultery is always wrong. Put
another way, 53% thought that adultery can be
justified, at least in certain circumstances.

In the same poll, only a tiny 2% said that drinking and
driving could ever be justified.

If a survey were done on what the Bible calls sexual
immorality, I should think the vast majority of people
would say that it can be justified in certain circumstances. That's assuming that anyone thought there was
anything to justify. The Bible's sexual standards aren't
exactly popular or fashionable, are they?

Yet the feelings of guilt and shame over our sexual
misconduct can be completely crippling. It's hard to
think of anything else, as we're only too aware of the
ways that we've messed things up, and we seriously
wonder whether there's any way back from here. It's
compounded by the fact that we are often facing it
alone, or at best with our partner. Most of us are not
confident of being able to tell someone older in our
church about the difficulties that we face.[1] We fear that
we'll be thought perverse if we admit to the degree of
struggle that we are going through. We dare not risk

the looks of horror, or worse, judgment, and we're probably embarrassed and ashamed. What we probably don't realize is that there is every chance that the person we're afraid to talk to has had problems of his or her own, and is likely to be sympathetic.

We are also ashamed because this is something that at least one other person in our life knows about. We have been more physically intimate than we should have been with our partner, and the shame that we feel (usually shared by our partner too) is worse because this other person knows what we're really like. In front of our friends we can usually put on masks and pretend to be a lot more respectable than we really are. Here, though, we've revealed to ourselves and to our partner that we aren't as great as we like to think we are. Or as great as we would like them to think we are.

Perhaps most crippling of all is the knowledge that often when we've overstepped the line that we had decided was sensible for our relationship, we've done it knowingly. We've done it because we've wanted to.[2] It's not that we've been so excited that we've completely lost control and found ourselves doing things before we've even realized they were happening. We've been excited, sure. But as the excitement has grown, so has our desire, and with it the temptation to carry on. We can't kid ourselves. Unless we've been very drunk, few of us can claim that we haven't known what we were doing. Temptation has got the better of us; we've decided to let go and overstep the boundary. We probably lost a degree of control, but, in the final analysis, we knew what the choice was, and we might well have felt uneasy about it at the time. Perhaps we sensed it was wrong but we continued anyway. The knowledge that we perhaps struggled with a situation and then made a decision that we knew to be wrong at the time is deeply shaming. We are left to wonder how we can ever put the pieces back together again.

Actually it is right that we feel a sense of guilt and shame. We are guilty, and what we have done has been shameful. As we stated at the outset, we are created in the image of God, and though it may be barely recognizable, we do still bear traces of his likeness. Part of that means that we are made to be in a relationship with God and to be like him in our character. None of us are very good at being godly. We all make a mess of it, but we are all nevertheless called by God to be holy in the same way that he is.[3] Being holy has nothing to do with wearing sandals and going to church; it has everything to do with being set apart for God – not necessarily in a monastery, but in everyday life. We're to live our lives in the world, but not be like most of the people in it. When we blow it and fail, we should feel shame and guilt. We've been guilty of what the Bible calls 'sin'. And we need to wage war on sin in our life, trying to live lives that are more and more pleasing to God. Sexual sins are sins, make no mistake about it. It's actually a positive thing to feel ashamed and sorry for the ways that we've made a mess of things in our sex lives, because this should provoke us to do something about it.

There are several options open to us when we decide to do something about sorting out our sex lives. To begin with, we might decide to redouble our efforts and buckle down to being good from now on. Trouble is, this doesn't tend to work. As we've already said, we have a tendency to fail time and time again. Gritting our teeth and trying harder doesn't have a very high success rate. Sometimes the whole thing becomes so messy and complicated that we decide to give up on the relationship altogether. We can't handle the way that the relationship is working out, so we hope that by knocking it on the head we can end our problems. Well, it does take away our immediate temptations and may or may not be a good idea at this stage. But we still have to face exactly the same situations if we go out with someone else at a later date. We need to lose the guilt we're living under, too.

All this guilt that we're feeling, wouldn't it be a lot easier if we just forgot all about it? No-one's perfect. We all make mistakes, and life's too short to spend crying over spilt milk. (Add any other appropriate clichés you can think of here!) Forgetting about it and starting again is attractive enough, but if we're trying to live as a Christian it's nigh on impossible. We try to read the Bible and words leap out at us which remind us of our guilt. We sit in church and feel miserable, even if we've managed to fool everyone there with our smiles. We don't seem to get anywhere when we try to pray; it's as if someone's stuck a great barrier between ourselves and God. If we decide that we simply want to try to forget it, the discomfort of trying to live a double life means that sooner or later one of our lives will crack. All too often it's the one that causes the most discomfort that will be dropped.

I've seen a frightening number of people give up on their faith for the attractions of a boy or girlfriend. The pressure becomes too great, and so it feels easier to live in a relationship with Chris or Jo(e) than it does with God. Please, don't give up on it. No relationship is more important than the one you have with God.

There is a better way. The reason it feels as though there is a barrier separating us from God is that there is one. The Bible talks about sin in this way. The things that we have got wrong and not done God's way separate us from God. The reason that we feel distant from God is because we *are* distant and, to make it worse, it's our fault. We feel bad about that. If we've been in a position where we've been enjoying a relationship with God, to lose that feels acutely uncomfortable. The bad news is that there isn't a lot that we can do by ourselves to get rid of the barrier and make a new start, however much we might like to be able to undo and reconstruct our past. The good news is that, while we can't shift the blockage ourselves, we can do something about getting rid of it.

You see, we aren't the only ones to feel bad about the distance that there is between ourselves and God when we make a mess of things. God feels it too. Astonishing though it may sound to us, we are so highly valued by God that he wants to have a relationship with us. Sexual sin separates us from him and, knowing that we are utterly powerless to do anything about the situation, God has solved the problem himself. He offers to forgive us for the ways that we've messed things up, and he gives us the chance to make a brand new start.

That offer of forgiveness isn't just restricted to sexual sin, of course. But it is one of the numerous ways in which we fall short of God's perfect standards every day. We don't tend to be so aware of many of the other ways in which we make a mess of things. We might be fairly proud about something we've done, or be rather condescending to other people, or tend to be quite jealous, or there could be any number of other ways in which we aren't as like Jesus as we should be. We can be blind to them all. This is especially the case if we are in the midst of a raging battle concerning our sexual behaviour with our partner. We are so aware of the ways that we fail in this area, and so keen to sort them out, that we don't even notice that we're gossiping or very critical of everyone we come into contact with.

This might be the hardest thing for you to believe as a Christian, but God can, and does, forgive us our sexual sins. This is hard to accept in a culture that will splash the adultery of a filmstar or sportsperson across the front pages of the tabloids. Even better if they can use their 'RANDY VICAR AND SUNDAY SCHOOL TEACHER SHOCK' headlines. The papers love this sort of thing – the chance to shout 'HYPOCRITE!' We hold on to this idea that any kind of sexual misbehaviour is the very worst way we can make a mess of our

Christian lives. The ways that we foul up sexually are not in a special category that is too difficult for God to cope with. Sure, they may be harder for *us* to cope with. We've caught a glimpse of the sort of person we really are: we're rebellious; we think we know best; we wonder how God can possibly forgive us. After all, we've been so bad.

Why are we so prone to think that Jesus is only interested in the nice and the respectable, the people who are naturally religious (whatever that means)? We think that Jesus is only concerned with the better people in the world. So if he knows as much about me as he says he does, he must be deeply unimpressed. He can't be interested or concerned about me.

This isn't a new point of view. The religious teachers of Jesus' time (the respectable ones) had serious doubts about Jesus because he spent so much time hanging out with 'sinners'. By this they meant what they'd call obvious sinners – prostitutes and tax collectors – not the more discreet and sophisticated sinners that we are. Their line of argument was the same way of thinking that we can lapse into: if Jesus knew what these people were really like, he wouldn't have had anything to do with them.

Jesus responded to the muttering of the religious teachers ('This man welcomes sinners, and eats with them')[4] in a way that most of us wouldn't even think of. I'd have been inclined to put them in their place, but Jesus tells them three stories, one after another.[5] The parable of a lost sheep, the parable of a lost coin, and the parable of a lost son. All three feature something being lost, being looked for, and then being found. And then there's a party afterwards to celebrate the safe recovery of the sheep, coin or son.

Some of Jesus' parables are more difficult to understand than others. I know for certain that these three parables are about the fact that Jesus is deeply and passionately concerned for lost people to be back in a relationship with him. I know this to be the case because Jesus tells us himself. He likens the sort of celebrations that happen at the finding of the missing coin to those that happen in heaven over a person who repents of his or her sin.[6] This is the case whether we are Christians or not, whether we consider ourselves respectable or not, and regardless of how we feel about whatever we have done. The attitude of Jesus to society's outcasts tells us that he cares for us no matter what, and is longing to see us turn around — back to him.

This is the central theme of the Bible and can be seen throughout it. Another time, when the religious teachers asked why he spent time with 'sinners', Jesus spoke of being there as a doctor for the sick.[7] Now unless the tax collectors and sinners that he was eating with were a particularly poorly bunch, Jesus couldn't have been talking about physical sickness. He goes on to explain that he was there to call sinners to him. In other words, his very mission was to heal each one of us who have made a mess of things, who have sinned and fallen short of God's standards for the way we should live our lives. We're all sick and in need of a doctor.

The Jesus who scandalized the religious authorities by being at parties with prostitutes isn't so appalled by the ways we've got our sex lives wrong that he can't associate with us. The vital and amazing truth that we must cling to is that God does forgive us. Sexual sin isn't further up the league table of sins than gossiping and lying. Yet we far more readily accept that we can ask for forgiveness for the latter; we can hardly believe that we can have the slate wiped clean in a far more personal area of our lives. Well, please do believe it! Sexual sins aren't more important or less forgivable than other forms of sin, and we will be forgiven them if we repent.

All this talk about repenting, it sounds dreadfully old-fashioned, doesn't it? Sounds like the sort of thing you'd expect to hear from an old-fashioned preacher. I use the word deliberately, though, because it's more than just saying sorry. We can feel sorry about doing something without feeling particularly repentant. Repentance is more active than feeling sorrow over our mistakes. There will be the element of being sorrowful, but repentance also represents a clear desire to be different in future. It involves turning around and heading in the opposite direction. In the context of our subject, it isn't just feeling bad about our sexual behaviour and wanting the past erased. It's also a desire to run from that kind of situation in the future.

Now the chances are that, because you've been so haunted by your mistakes, it will be all the motive that you need to repent. Once we have finally and truly got it into our heads that we can be forgiven, we will soon be praying and asking God for his forgiveness. To repent isn't too much of a problem. We know how we've messed things up, how it's made us feel, how it's hurt someone else, and we don't want it to happen again. What is likely to be harder, however, is to *accept* that we have been forgiven. We might find it hard to believe that God forgives us, and even when it's in our heads we don't necessarily feel it in our hearts. It all seems too good to be true. So the temptation is to keep on asking God to forgive us. We come back to him asking to be forgiven again because somehow we can't quite believe that he'll have mercy on us; we're such dreadful people. And of course we are, but he's forgiven us just the same. We must take God at his word. Even if we can't forgive ourselves, God can. He isn't hard of hearing, nor does he forgive us a piece at a time. If you ask a second time to be forgiven for any one incident, you're really wasting your breath. God's done it already.

In his first letter to the churches, John makes this promise of forgiveness clear. As people who regularly make a mess of things, we need to be familiar with these words. Indeed, some churches use these words every week, and if you are so familiar with them that they've lost any meaning for you as a result, then you need to let them hit you with their original force. Read the wider passage that this comes from, 1 John 1:5 – 2:6. It'll do you good. The verses that are the crux of the issue for us are these:

If we claim to be without sin, we deceive ourselves and the truth is not in us. If we confess our sins, he is faithful and just and will forgive us our sins and purify us from all unrighteousness.[8]

The Bible contains this great promise that God forgives us when we ask him. There's no footnote to say 'unless you've been really rude'. Neither is there a PS that says 'unless you've been rude in this way before and you've blown it again, in which case you're on your own. Tough, you've had your chance.' No, it says, 'If we confess our sins, he is faithful and just and will forgive us our sins and purify us ...' This is a fantastic truth that we need to grasp and thankfully hold on to.

Since repentance is more than saying sorry and involves turning from the things that we have done, it would be sensible to look now at how we can think practically about making that 180 degree turn. Temptation will raise its ugly head again, of that we can be sure. How will we respond when it does? Oscar Wilde famously wrote in *Lady Windermere's Fan* that it's possible to resist everything except temptation. Are we going to be in the same sinking boat? If we're repenting, we need to work out how we'll fight the temptation that we'll face to repeat our mistakes.

Some of the things that follow will make me sound like your parent, but I don't care. Some of it has been passed on by people who have already been there, done that, got the tee shirt, and then regretted it horribly and been messed up by it. In the questionnaires that I circulated while researching this book, one of the most useful comments I received came from someone who offered this thought:

> *'The advice may indeed seem hard but it's just so true —*
> *learn from other's mistakes rather than your own!'*

So many of the people who have got it wrong and have regrets would want to pass this on: 'Don't make the mistakes that I made, learn from the mess that I'm in. You really don't want to be here, badly hurt with regrets.'

These people have come through it, though, as wiser people. Here's a chance to learn from them. Some of this will seem painfully obvious, but some of the problems that we run up against are brought about precisely because we ignore the obvious. We think that we don't need to concern ourselves with it. We're cleverer than that. That sort of basic advice is for other people. But we ignore it at our peril, however old-fashioned and basic it might at first appear. One of the most poignant comments that the survey yielded was from someone who knew what the advice was all along but admitted, 'I felt I knew better.' That's the trouble, isn't it? We think that we know better.

Here, then, is some practical advice to help you work all this out in your life.

First, there is no point in thinking about how far you will be going in your physical relationship with your girl or boyfriend if you don't communicate your thoughts to them. This is equally the case whether you are in a long-running relationship or starting to see someone for the first time. It's vital that you are not only talking together but also communicating – there's a great difference. It might be that you feel so embarrassed about this shared area of failure that you would rather talk about anything else, but it has to be done. If you've become convinced that there are things that you shouldn't be doing in your relationship, then you need to talk this through with your partner. If this is clear from the start, then there is less scope for confusion and for feeling rejection later on in the relationship. Each knows where they stand, and that they stand together. This is an enormously positive start to a relationship. You both have shared values, and will be battling together rather than against each other.

The second point is that, if you drink, you need to watch how much. We all know that alcohol clouds our judgment, and we know that we don't always make great decisions when we have had a few drinks. How many is too many will vary between individuals, but if you're going out for the night and don't want to do something that you'll regret later, you need to give a night in the bar or club some forward thought. Before you leave the house, think about how much you'll drink during the evening. Set yourself a sensible limit knowing what you will be like if you exceed it. Then stick to it, whatever the pressures to do otherwise. Lots of people have found it difficult to go out and see so many attractive people, knowing that some of them will have gone out solely with the intention of picking someone up. They know that they could probably get a result if they tried hard enough. If you are facing that temptation, then it will be much harder to resist if you've been drinking. Similarly, if you're out on a date and have had a few drinks and are feeling relaxed, it's lot easier to go along with what you are feeling than what your head tells you is wise.

Thirdly, you need to avoid lying down together. This is one of those times where the truth is so obvious that it seems facile. But it's good advice all the same, which a significant number of people would want to pass on. It's much easier to get carried away if you are lying down, much easier to start touching things you shouldn't and taking off clothing. You don't tend to lie down with many people generally in life, so the very act is itself one which suggests greater intimacy. You obviously want to keep your clothes on too – even partial undressing is really unwise. (OK, you may not *want* to keep your clothes on, but you should!) This is simpler in the winter in a draughty shared house than in the summer when we wear a lot less anyway. A lot of blokes have a big enough problem as it is with the things that some women just about wear in the summer; we tend to be stimulated by the visual, hence the struggle so many of us have with pornography. In the same way that men need to be aware that women are generally more aroused by touch and should be careful how they act as a result, women need to know that men are turned on by the sight of a well-turned ankle (and more), and need to bear that in mind. Men and women are under enough temptation, without adding to it.

The next couple of things are particularly important if you are living in a single room in a shared house or on a corridor. In a situation like that, it's hard to find a bit of privacy. Many of us have no access to a living-room and may only have a kitchen as a communal space. There will be times when you don't particularly want to be conducting your conversations in that kitchen, and so to have a bit of privacy you go to your room. Your room of course has a bed in it. Maybe you decide to lie down, and that can lead to boundaries being broken. It might sound hopelessly cautious, but you know that it happens. A simple way to help fight that kind of temptation is to keep the door to your room open. It's a powerful encouragement to keep your clothes on if you don't know who will be walking past at any moment!

Another problem with having just one room to live in is what do you do when a boy or girlfriend comes to stay? Or what do you do late at night when they have a few miles to walk home? The easiest thing in the world is to let them stay over for the night. Regardless of whether this puts you under added temptation or not, and all the chances are that it does, it isn't the best idea in the world. When I was in a hall of residence at college, I had a friend visit for the weekend. It wasn't a romantic relationship, we were just friends, and I didn't even think about the consequences of her sleeping in my room. Until later, when the other guys on my corridor gave me huge amounts of stick for it. They knew that I was a Christian. They knew that I'd had a woman living in my room for a weekend. The conclusion that they drew was that I was a hypocrite. They knew that Christians shouldn't do what they assumed I'd been doing. It was virtually a waste of breath trying to talk to them about God for the rest of the year. Looking back, I wish I'd been wise enough to arrange for her to stay with one of my female friends. It would have saved a lot of misunderstanding.

One more thing of great value in all this is very scary to most of us. It's about having the kind of friendship with someone of the same sex where it's possible to share your struggles, give each other support, and pray together. This obviously involves us in being vulnerable and open with each other, as there's not a lot of point in meeting up together and then avoiding the issue. You need to exercise some care here. If only one partner in a relationship has this kind of friendship then tensions can arise: 'What is he or she saying about me?' But this kind of deep friendship with someone of the same sex is extremely valuable.

I've found it to be of enormous benefit to be in this kind of accountable relationship. You need to give each other permission to ask difficult questions about how you are doing in terms of the physical side of your relationship with your girl/boyfriend. This requires us to screw up some courage, and is particularly difficult for men who would much rather make a commitment to meet once a week to talk about football. I certainly found it tempting to do just that! But I also found it deeply helpful to be talking to another bloke about how we were both doing in this area of our lives and to be praying together for each other.

That final point is one that I've assumed all the way through: the role of prayer. We know all too well that we aren't the strongest people in the world in the area of resisting sexual temptation. One of the great things about being a Christian is that when we do feel a bit feeble, we are more likely to pray. This doesn't just make us feel better after having talked to someone about it, it helps us immeasurably more. Because God promises us his help in the battle that we're in, we aren't alone in this. It doesn't guarantee us an instant victory and deliverance from sexual temptation, because we are still people with freedom to make our own decisions, but God's help is a vital weapon in the battle that we're engaged in. If we want to live by God's standards in our sex lives, it makes great sense to ask for God's help in that fight. That of course applies to every area of our life – don't become so concentrated on this area of your life that you are ignorant of the other ones that you need to work on. Pray with someone in an accountable same-sex friendship, pray with your partner, pray on your own. Pray.

This isn't easy advice to follow; you're in for some serious hard work. It's tempting to do nothing about the problem because in the short term it avoids the need to address the situation. But the longer things drift, the more painful it is in the end. The advice is given to help you fight temptation and to work at being in a healthy relationship with your boy/girlfriend. You might already be in the kind of relationship where you are struggling to keep to the boundaries that you set. If you're falling down in this way, you need to sort it out. The way that has been outlined is to seek the forgiveness that God offers, the chance to make a fresh start.

As a couple, you need to repent together, and to work and pray at building a healthy relationship, one which avoids the sexual immorality that the Bible warns against. Be warned, it won't be easy. Once boundaries are broken they are more easily broken a second or third time. Living a new life with a lifestyle to match, even as forgiven people, isn't easy. But it's possible. It isn't unattainable because God promises us his help in the struggle.

Some people, however, will find that the struggle is too much for them. They are in an unhealthy relationship and are unable to turn it into something healthy. They will try not to lie down together, they will try to stay dressed, but temptation gets the better of them each time.

If you're in a relationship like this, you need to do some hard thinking. You can carry on getting it wrong, struggling from failure to failure, but this will do neither of you any good and will probably do you long-lasting damage. It isn't a healthy option.

So far as I can see, you really only have three options. It would help you to think them through with someone.

One option is to avoid that kind of temptation by getting married. Then you can have as much sex as you want. This might be an option for you, but it might be disastrous. Don't rush into marriage just to avoid the mess of sex outside marriage. Sex isn't recommended as the basis for a relationship! Pursuing this option might just be a way of trying to avoid working through a very difficult and painful issue.

We've already looked at the second option. Talk to your partner and sort it out once and for all. As we've recognized, this is exceptionally difficult. You need to strive together to avoid acting sexually in your relationship. You might well need to find someone older and wiser to help you work through your problems. Even then it won't be easy, but it is possible.

On the other hand, there is the one last option that you probably don't want to consider at all. It might be tough, but if you are in bad relationship, which causes you pain and does you great harm, then you need to consider this option seriously. If you can't turn your bad relationship into a good one, you need to end that relationship. It probably sounds cold-hearted to issue such a stark challenge, but it's far better that you make a decision like this before you are committed in a marriage relationship. It's a decision that a lot of people wish they had taken earlier than they did.

This isn't the negative advice that it might at first sight appear. The experience of God's forgiveness and the desire to make a fresh start can revolutionize life. The chances are that being in a bad relationship has made it extremely difficult for you to spend much time with God. You try to pray and read the Bible but you keep coming across passages that point out that your behaviour in your relationship is less than what God wants for you. It becomes uncomfortable to read the Bible, hard work to pray, and soon there doesn't seem a lot of point in trying. Church is a hard place to be too. Perhaps it becomes a place to avoid, because you feel a bit of a hypocrite singing those songs. Well, to pull something positive out of the experience, here is an opportunity to spend time again in studying the Bible and prayer. And a time to get back into church, perhaps to renew some neglected friendships too. Don't miss the opportunity to get involved in a friendship that will help you see life in a wider perspective. It will be better than sitting at home thinking that everyone else is one of a couple and that you're a social leper.

'Reader, I married him.'

Jane Eyre, *Charlotte Bronte*

Have you ever played a board game called 'The Game of Life'? Someone gave me one as a present, and the first time I played it I wasn't sure whether to be appalled or amused. The idea of the game is to pass through the various stages of life, from education right through to retirement. The winner (naturally enough) is the person who makes the most money. After all, that's what life is all about. More shocking, though, is one of the squares that you have to stop at. Fairly early in the game, between your first job and acquiring a mortgage, you must get married. You have no choice in the matter, it's compulsory. All the other players give you £1,000 as a wedding present (the game is very life-like) and you get a pink or blue peg to add to the plastic car that acts as your counter. You then carry on around the board, all the time aiming to retire in order to count your savings.

This chapter isn't written in that spirit! In talking about marriage in a book on friendship and relationships, I am not assuming that marriage is a stage that we will all 'progress' to at some point. I'm not for a moment even saying that we all should, either! But having underlined the importance of keeping sex exclusively for the marriage relationship, it's sensible to think a little about what happens when we make that kind of commitment to another person. In particular, is there any advantage to getting married rather than just living together?

A lot of my friends haven't bothered to get married, or they've lived together for a long time first. They've read the figures that are regularly in the papers about the breakdown of marriage, they see the divorce statistics and conclude, with the odds already stacked against them: Why bother taking the plunge? Why take all that trouble to arrange a wedding? Why spend all that money just for a piece of paper? You can hardly blame them; it seems like a pretty persuasive argument.

There's no doubt that a wedding can be a great source of stress. Suddenly there are major decisions to be made – including really vital ones, like the shape of the cake and the exact colour the bridesmaids should be wearing! There are people who you do not, under any circumstances, want to sit next to each other at the reception for fear of a small war breaking out. There are the distant cousins that you last saw at a family wedding several years ago (what are their names again?) – do you invite them? There are so many decisions to be made, and everyone has an opinion: your family, your partner's family, friends, hairdressers, the lot. Some of these unimportant decisions suddenly seem critical if we're so enamoured with the romance of the wedding day that everything has to be just perfect. You certainly won't please everyone, in fact there are times when it'll seem nothing short of miraculous that *anyone* is happy with all the arrangements.

In a survey that was undertaken to establish the amount of stress associated with the big events of life, researchers Holmes and Rahe came up with an interesting league table.[1] It's probably no surprise to learn that the most stressful event in life is the death of a spouse. It rates 100 points on the scale. Second to this is divorce, rating 73 points. Marriage is just down the list at 50 points (I think the researchers are referring to getting married rather than being married). It's rated as being more stressful than the death of a close friend, being sacked at work, retirement or even sexual difficulties – which rate 39 points. No wonder you need a honeymoon to relax a bit afterwards, although be warned that a holiday is rated at 13 points! If you haven't lived together beforehand, it'll cost you 25 points to adjust to living together too. When you begin to add up everything that you might experience in the year that you get married, you become aware of how close you can get to the 150 points that the researchers rather dramatically call a 'life crisis'. What they mean is that you are more likely to become ill as a result of all the changes that you experience, be they good or bad ones.

Well, there's a good reason not to get married! Here's another one. It's so expensive! Annually, someone does a survey of how much the 'average wedding' costs the happy couple. I seriously wonder what planet these people live on, because I find it hard to believe that I've ever been to the kind of wedding that they are talking about. But I'll bet I've been to a number. Where (on earth?) do these surveys get such astronomical figures from? To add to the confusion, they can't seem to agree on the figures. In one weekend I read figures from two separate sets of research that had tried to cost the big day.[2] According to *Wedding and Home* magazine the average amount spent on a wedding is £8,653, while *You and Your Wedding* magazine makes it a suspiciously round-figured £11,500. Not much of a discrepancy there then! The difference between the figures would go a long way to paying for a wedding. Even if you're sensible about the amount that you pay out on the big day and honeymoon, there's no doubt that you're talking about a serious outlay. (There is, of course, no correlation between the cost of a wedding and how enjoyable it is.) But why put up all that cash when the statistics tell us there is a good chance of it all ending in tears anyway?[3]

The figures on divorce, terrible though they undoubtedly are, only tell us part of the story, however. By focusing on the statistics for marital breakdown, we can miss the fact that each year thousands and thousands of couples marry. They find deep friendship, security and pleasure in marriage, and they are very happy to remain married. This is easily overlooked.

Other people want to get married, but they take one look at the figures quoted and instantly know they cannot afford those kinds of prices, and won't be able to do so for a good number of years. You only do it once, so surely it's far better to save up and spend the first chunk of money on a deposit for somewhere to live and get married later. To start with, you can save faster when you're only paying one lot of rent, or just one mortgage. Yet to do so puts you at a serious disadvantage in the marriage stakes. The statistics tell us, perhaps surprisingly, that you have more chance of being divorced if you have already lived together before marriage – in fact, the risk is increased by 50%.[4]

Others are understandably cynical about getting married, due to what they've seen in the marriages of others, often those of their parents. Whilst we all have these ideals in our heads about couples living happily ever after, we only have to look at many marriages to see that the theory and the practice are miles apart. It's well known that a growing number of marriages end in divorce, and there are also countless marriages that are marriages only in name. Any sense of togetherness, mutuality and intimacy that were expressed at the altar died long ago. For many of us this is a very good reason to skip getting married and simply live together. It's cheaper, less stressful and safer all round. So, fewer of us bother to take the plunge these days: 400,435 couples in 1973; 344,334 in 1983; 299,197 ten years after that.[5]

We have to recognize that, sadly, many marriages seem rather shallow and aren't great advertisements for the institution. And, as one of the Marx brothers said, 'Marriage is a great institution but who wants to live in an institution?' We look at some of the marriages around us and they do not inspire us to tie the knot. But they should also show us that the old cliché that the

marriage contract is just a piece of paper is a false one.
The problems that we are capable of giving to one
another within a marriage relationship demonstrate all
too clearly that there is a great deal more to marriage
than simply getting a piece of paper.

When we choose to get married, we make the most
enormous promises. If we get married in an Anglican
church, for instance, we promise to cleave to our spouse,

> for better, for worse,
> for richer, for poorer,
> in sickness and in health,
> to love and to cherish,
> till death us do part.[6]

And that's only the start of it! At various points in the
service husband and wife promise to love, comfort, hon-
our and protect one another. They promise to forsake all
others and be faithful to each other as long as they both
shall live. The couple promise to share all that they have
with each other. No wonder the service starts with a
warning not to enter into marriage lightly, carelessly or
selfishly, but after doing some serious thinking. These
are big promises that you are making to each other. More
significantly, you make them in front of your families
and friends. Even more significantly, in the case of the
sort of marriage service that we've just quoted from,
these are promises that we consciously make before God.
That has been particularly significant for some couples;
it has been the only thing that has kept some together

during the struggles they've encountered in their marriage. Often this has been during the first year, when they are having to make enormous changes as they start living together. These promises that we make are ones which we know, if we've thought at all deeply about them, will be extraordinarily difficult to keep on our own, and we need God's help. I certainly remember saying a quick prayer at the altar! You look at the radical promises that you make at the wedding and quickly realize that marriage is the ultimate commitment. Much more than a piece of paper or a legal contract, marriage is to be a lifetime's commitment to one another.

In case you haven't already guessed, this isn't an easy undertaking. As well as being aware of God's help through prayer as we do this, we can turn to the Bible to get good guidelines for what this commitment means in the course of everyday living with each other.

At first glance, one of the strangest things that we do during the marriage ceremony is to promise to love one another until 'death us do part'. How can we possibly promise that? Feelings change; how do we know that we'll feel the same way about our partners in twenty days' time, let alone twenty years? Well, the simple answer is that we don't. In fact, it's very unlikely that we'll feel exactly the same way about our spouse in five, ten, or fifty years' time.

It would be rather strange if we did. As you get to know your husband or wife over a period of time (because, believe me, you'll discover all sorts of things about each other as you start to inhabit the same living space!), you'll appreciate new things about them as well as discover some (more?) things that annoy you. Unbelievably, they are discovering faults in you too! As with all good relationships, your marriage should develop. But, even as you develop, you are still able to keep up that commitment to love each other – because the sort of love that we are talking about here isn't the insipid stuff of Mills and Boon novels. It's not the romantic myth of 'happy ever after'. It's a far more robust love than that. It's a love that recognizes that sometimes a relationship is a battle, but that it's worth fighting for.

The ancient Greeks had several words for love, whereas we have just the one. I may love David Bowie, pork and ginger with cashew nuts, a beer, Barton Fink, the Beano and my wife. I can assure you, however, that I don't love them all in the same way. The Greeks wouldn't have had these problems with the word 'love', nor such scope for confusion. When they talked about erotic love or friendship love, they were able to use different words that made the distinction clear. They had a particularly potent word for one form of love, *agape*. This was used for the kind of love that isn't always deserved. It is love expressed to us whether we deserve it or not. It means that we love a person because we recognize that person has intrinsic worth, regardless of whether he or she is particularly lovely or not. 'Agape love' is a love that extends to another person in spite of the person, not because that person inspires warm feelings in us for him or her. It's a committed love, whatever the circumstances may be.

Well, good for the Greeks! The thing is, the New Testament was written in Greek, and the kind of love that Christians were urged to practise was this *agape* love. Not loving people because they are nice, but loving them in spite of the fact that they will sometimes send us round the bend. That's an enduring love! It's not the sort of love that we naturally find ourselves dispensing. But it's what true love is all about. It isn't the pink hearts and flowers of romantic love; it's the unsentimental love that has decided it's going to hold on whatever the situation. This is why we are able to promise to love each other for our shared lifetime – because we are committed to sticking together through thick and thin (and thinner). We might need to remind ourselves of the fact sometimes and renew those promises, but the bottom line is that we are making the decision to love for life. That's the rugged love that the Bible talks about.

Perhaps the most famous discussion in the Bible about love is the one that talks about this *agape* love. With the kind of sexual immorality that we've seen going on in Corinth, it's perhaps no great surprise to find that it's to the church at Corinth that Paul chooses to write about true *agape* love and what it's all about. This is a well-known passage that gets read at a lot of weddings, and here it is in a modern translation:

> Love never gives up.
> Love cares more for others than for self.
> Love doesn't want what it doesn't have.

> Love doesn't strut,
> Doesn't have a swelled head,
> Doesn't force itself on others,
> Isn't always 'me first',
> Doesn't fly off the handle,
> Doesn't keep score of the sins of others,
> Doesn't revel when others grovel,
> Takes pleasure in the flowering of truth,
> Puts up with anything,
> Trusts God always,
> Always looks for the best,
> Never looks back,
> But keeps going to the end.
> Love never dies.[7]

Read that passage again. To read about that kind of love is breathtaking, isn't it? This isn't the stuff of the romantic novel where two people finally get married and live happily ever after. In those books the goal is to get married; once you've walked down the aisle everything is worked out. What we know, of course, is that the wedding day is just the beginning of it all. God's book doesn't sell you any romantic delusions. It acknowledges that living together isn't always a picnic, and that you need to demonstrate this kind of love to one another all the time. It's *agape* love.

Now this type of love isn't just something that is confined to the marriage relationship. It's the kind of love that all Christians are called to demonstrate. We know all too well that we constantly fail in this, but we

should be demonstrating *agape* love in all our relationships, within families and friendships. No wonder we
need God's help! When we are talking about marriage,
we see that we are setting the very highest standards for
that relationship. Nor does it end there. There's plenty
more on marriage that we find in the Bible, some of
which has caused a great deal of confusion. Let's look at
one of those passages.

The Bible has sometimes been accused of being sexist
in its attitudes. Actually, when we consider the radical
attitude that Jesus displayed towards women, in complete contrast to the rest of his culture, it would be
more accurate to say that it is Paul who is accused of
being sexist, or worse, misogynist! Here's a passage that
gets a few hackles rising:

> *Wives, submit to your husbands as to the Lord. For the hus-
> band is the head of the wife as Christ is the head of the
> church, his body, of which he is the Saviour. Now as the
> church submits to Christ, so also wives should submit to
> their husbands in everything.*[8]

There you are, what further proof could you ever need
for the sort of attitude that we've been talking about?
Well, there's a great deal that can be said about these
verses, and about women's roles in the church in general. There are several books' worth of material here,
and we simply don't have the space to go into it in
depth. What we can say here, first of all, is that submitting to a husband as to the Lord does not mean

blind obedience to a tyrannical (or even benevolent) dictator. Wives are not expected to submit to anything that is contrary to what God commands. There will be times when the husband is quite clearly wrong. It is even likely that he will be thankful to his wife later for the discernment that she showed in refusing to go along with something that was unbiblical. Secondly, there is this whole vexed issue of 'headship'. We tend to read this word and equate it with the male being in charge, yet nowhere in this passage is the word 'authority' (*exousia*) used.[9] As John Stott points out in his very helpful analysis of this passage, Christ's headship of the church 'expresses care rather than control, responsibility rather than rule'.[10]

So headship means the husband caring for and having responsibility for his wife. Wives are to submit to instruction from the husband, providing that such counsel is scriptural. In addition to this, we'd do well to read the passage in context. Paul goes on to instruct husbands to 'love your wives, just as Christ loved the church and gave himself up for her ...'[11] This is astonishing: husbands are instructed to love their wives in the same way that Christ loves the church! – to the extent of laying down their lives for them. These words are radical enough for today, let alone in a culture where women were mere possessions and had no legal rights whatsoever. This is hardly one-way traffic, with the husband laying down the law and the wife meekly obeying his every instruction.

Finally, if we look at the sentence that precedes the

passage we've glanced at, we find the instruction, 'submit to one another out of reverence for Christ'.[12] Whilst some translations of the Bible, such as the New International Version, have attached this to the previous section of the letter, others see the instruction as applying to what follows. It makes a great deal of sense that Paul starts with this instruction ('submit to one another') and then goes on to demonstrate how the principle is worked out in practice, with men and women submitting to each other in marriage.

We are instructed to love one another with an *agape* love. It's a radical, enduring, rugged, unsentimental, tough love. It calls us to commit ourselves to loving each other regardless of the circumstances. We see that this will involve submitting to each other. When we get married, we are committing ourselves to a lifetime of this. Do you see now why marriage is so much more than a legal contract?

I am concerned for friends who just want to settle for living together. Some of them are honest enough to admit that they aren't ready for the kind of commitment that marriage requires. For the reasons that have already been outlined, sex is safest in an environment of complete commitment. And, in this environment of commitment, we are free to be open and intimate in other ways within marriage. Marriage offers this in a way that no other arrangement does, because in getting married you publicly promise to be committed to your partner for life, come what may. That commitment is the *foundation* of the marriage. It says that, regardless of what might happen, whatever might go wrong in our lives, we are pledged to one another. We'll fight as one flesh, together.

This is tremendously liberating. It brings a freedom from fear of getting it all wrong. If we are pledged to each other, we have less to fear for the consequences of making mistakes. We will make mistakes, we're all too human. But the commitment that we make to each other should ensure that the relationship has an underlying stability. The bottom line is that we are committed to each other and not just our own individual interests.

If we are committed to a lifetime together, we have the security of knowing that both of us are determined to support the other. We can establish common goals and plan for the future. This gives us a far better context, for instance, for having children. We are able to provide each other with emotional support, in a safer and more permanent environment than that of just living together. Our relationship can weather unexpected storms – such as redundancy, bereavement and illness. But more than that, we are engaged in a lifelong discovery of knowing and understanding each other better. We grow and develop together.

Viewed in this light, marriage is a radical step. No wonder that we need to be loving one another with an *agape* love. We see here a whole list of benefits to getting married. We also can't fail to be struck by the effort and commitment that need to be poured into the marriage relationship. Earlier we were talking about needing to work at friendship. This is even more the case in marriage. If you are thinking of getting married because of the romance of the big day, the chance to be the centre of attention and think that you'll automatically live happily ever after – forget it. The security isn't in *being* married; it's in working at *staying* married. Both parties have to be committed to working at that.

Even in the best of relationships where the couple choose instead to cohabitate, there isn't the commitment that we should see in marriage – because people who simply live together haven't pledged themselves to each other for ever, come what may. If a couple go through a bad patch and find themselves arguing a bit, there's nothing there to stop one of them from packing up and leaving. Many of these arrangements aren't necessarily permanent, anyway. When every disagreement potentially shifts the status of the relationship and necessitates a re-negotiation of the ground rules, you are in a precarious position. The relationship is all the more fragile because no-one has made a lifelong commitment to anyone. That's hardly a secure environment in which to be open and vulnerable with someone, and it is no foundation on which to build a future together.

One of the messages that comes over loud and clear in the film *Four Weddings and a Funeral* is that marriage isn't really up to much. In fact the byline that advertised the film read 'Five good reasons to stay single'. That might strike you as a strange thing to say, but next time you watch the film, ask yourself, 'What does this tell me about marriage?' The film even ends with the 'romantic scene' between Hugh Grant and Andie McDowell where they promise to live together and not get married. In fact, Hugh Grant's character asks for a commitment to *not* being committed in marriage! It's the sort of confused situation that allows them to share a life together, and bring children into the world, but without legally pledging themselves to each other for the rest of their lives. That seems a particularly unstable basis for a relationship in view of the findings of researchers, who tell us that men who are cohabiting are far more likely to be having sex with more than one partner than are married men or even older single men.[13] And, given the track record of the characters in the film, you'd have thought it would have been wise to get it in writing. I fear for the child they had!

There are some couples, of course, who live together and are happily committed to one another, are faithful, and have been so for years. But they still remain unmarried. To be honest, it might look to us as if some of these relationships work a lot better than many of the marriages that we see around us. Yet even to these people I would want to ask, why haven't you got married? You are married in all but name anyway, you say that you are committed to one another and that you plan on remaining monogamous and faithful. But that's exactly what marriage is all about. What's stopping you from making those promises publicly? For some there is a fear that once you are married the relationship will change, the magic will disappear, you'll take each other for granted, and perhaps you'll suddenly become like your parents! The standards that we've already laid down from the Bible about the quality of *agape* love that we should practise within all our relationships, and certainly within marriage, should be challenging enough for us to avoid that trap.

Having seen what an enormous commitment marriage is, we can see why it's not to be undertaken without some serious thought. If we thought about it in terms of sitting down and putting our signature to a lifelong commitment, I'm sure that even fewer of us would take the plunge. As it is, some of us drift into it as the next stage of our relationship or because we don't want to end up on the shelf, giving it about as much thought as signing a credit agreement for a hi-fi. It's a much bigger decision than that. Paul writes to the church at Corinth that, on balance, it's best to stay single if you can, although he certainly didn't ban anyone from getting married.[14]

This is quite a radical view in comparison to the emphasis that exists in our society for everyone to be part of a couple. Those of us who are single tend to be looked down on and treated as second-class citizens by some. You're thought of as a bit strange, and people might call into question your sexual orientation. Churches might be so family-orientated that they don't cater for single people in the congregation. I know of a number of single people who feel alienated to the point of leaving. Neither is it unknown to joke about the gift of singleness in terms which make it clear that we regard it as a curse. It's the gift that no-one wants.

Yet the degree of commitment that marriage requires

of both parties underlines that it's a bad idea to get married on the sole basis that someone has asked you. Much more thought is required. You need to be able to answer questions regarding how compatible you both are in terms of your personalities, interests, and with regard to what you aim to do with your lives. You also need to be able to handle the conflict that will inevitably be a part of your married life at some point or another, and you have to be able to communicate with each other. These two factors, the inability to communicate and being unable to handle conflict, have been identified as the biggest signs that a relationship won't work.[15] If when you disagree you only trade insults, or alternatively withdraw and sulk and refuse to talk about it, then you're in for trouble.

Being able to say 'no' to marriage is important, and a lot of the single people that I know have done that. Whilst our twisted worldview says that there's something wrong with men and women who don't get married, we need to emphasize that the 'one flesh' that the Bible talks about is made up of two whole people. Single people are not 'half persons'. Writing to the Corinthians, Paul recommends that those who are unmarried stay that way so that they can concentrate on pleasing God.[16] He points out that those who marry should take seriously their responsibility to their spouse, and will therefore have less time and energy to devote to God. We've already observed that Paul doesn't forbid marriage, but here we see that he doesn't exactly encourage it either. He recognizes that there are pros and cons to being married and to being single, which is more than most people in our society are prepared to admit. Today some see a single person and perhaps feel a little bit of pity for them. They assume that they must be lonely and unfulfilled.

It seems doubtful that Paul was married, of course, and in the face of the troubles that he went through – being imprisoned, flogged, beaten, ship-wrecked and constantly under threat for preaching about Jesus – being married would not have been helpful to his way of life.[17] Yet there's no way that you could say that he was living some sort of second-rate life. It was because he was single that he was able to do all that he did.

C. T. Studd was an English test cricketer who gave up everything to spread the gospel in Africa in the nineteenth century. Gordon MacDonald tells of hearing his story while he was a student, and thinking how impressive it was that Studd left his homeland and didn't see it for seventeen years as he went about his work. The trouble is, he didn't see his wife for that period of time either. She stayed in England to help their missionary organization there. It becomes more bizarre! After seventeen years his wife visited various missionaries in Africa to find out how the work was going. As part of the tour, she visited her husband for about half an hour. They talked about the progress of the mission and prayed together. Then she got back in her boat and sailed on to visit the next person on her list. As MacDonald observes, 'I still admire C. T. Studd, but not his perspective on marriage.'[18]

The wedding service summarizes the attitude with which we go into marriage: we make pledges to one another in public, and before God, which are for life. They aren't promises that can be made lightly. You hear the story of C. T. Studd and cannot help thinking that he would have been better off single, given how little his partnership with his wife must have come to mean. When thinking about marriage, we need to consider whether we should be married or not – not just assume that we should and then reduce it down to the question 'Who?'

9. from despair to where?

We started off by talking about Generation X and the sense of meaninglessness and alienation felt by so many of us born since 1961. That sense of aloneness, as we saw when we looked at loneliness, is at odds with the way that we were made to be. We are created to enjoy friendships and relationships, and we've been challenged by the standards of friendship that we should be setting as Christians. This is particularly difficult for us if we are trying to work out our relationships against a background where we are desperate for intimacy and yet we have been hurt by previous encounters. As a result, we often shy away from a full-blooded commitment to a person for fear of being hurt.

Then we began to think about what happens if we want to take a friendship with a member of the opposite sex further and start going out as a couple. We had a look at what the Bible has to say about the safest way to go out with someone, and the best way truly to get to know them, by not getting involved in a sexual relationship. This is strange behaviour as far as most people in our society are concerned, and in a culture where people are yearning for intimacy we often make the mistake of thinking that a sexual relationship is where we'll find it. The temptation to seek the acceptance and intimacy and security that we are looking for in a physical romantic relationship is strong.

We've also been made keenly aware of the great cost attached to the mistakes that we have made in our relationships as single people. Most of us have known the damage of inappropriate sexual behaviour outside of marriage, which the Bible starkly refers to as sexual immorality, a form of sin. However, we have also seen that there is a way out of the mess: the forgiveness that God offers us. The problem is, this is made all the more difficult for us to believe when one of the marks of X-ers is to disbelieve and dismiss the big promises that the Bible (or anyone else) makes. On top of that we are suspicious of the way that Christianity claims to make sense of the whole of life by offering, as it does, a coherent over-all explanation.

Finally, we've looked at why marriage is the best institution for working out a relationship, offering the security of a stated lifelong commitment to one another. This takes work, and is in many ways the beginning of the adventure rather than the happy ending it's often painted as.

It's interesting that the analogy of marriage is used in the Bible for the relationship between God and his people. That's another indication of the importance that the Bible attaches to marriage. The church itself is referred to as 'the bride of Christ'. Those who turn their backs on God and pursue other goals are referred to in terms of having committed adultery.[1]

As with a marriage relationship, the relationship that we have with God needs to be worked at and maintained. It's all too easy to let that slip when there's a flesh-and-blood person in our life who we find ourselves completely besotted by. We can quickly lose our sense of perspective and elevate our partners to ludicrous and dangerous heights in our estimation. It's a subtle form of idolatry; we're giving someone else our devotion rather than God.

There now follows a health warning: don't expect that one special person to fulfil all your expectations, or they'll buckle under the weight of them. Don't project on to them all the hopes and dreams that you have for a better life. Don't expect them to be able to provide for all your physical and emotional needs. In short, don't look to your partner for the things that only God can supply for you.

In looking at the whole subject of intimacy in what is largely a guarded world, we've been concentrating on human relationships, and we've been seeking to do them God's way. Yet, essentially, we must remember that the search for intimacy will never be fully satisfied by a flesh-and-blood partner. It can only be filled by a relationship with God, because as well as being created for relationships with other people, we were created for a relationship with him. From the beginning this was the way that it was meant to be. God walked and talked with Adam and Eve in the garden. They had a relationship with him.

But that relationship was spoiled when the created decided to live in a way that was different to that prescribed by the Creator. God told them not to touch some of the fruit in the garden, but man and woman decided that they knew better and, after all, rules are made to be broken, aren't they? This disobedience and decision to live life by their own rules (which the Bible describes as sin) meant that the relationship they had was spoiled. There was now a distance between God and his people.[2]

This is still the case. There's a distance between us and God, and as a result people even doubt that he exists. We live our lives without any reference to him. Most of us try to be good people, and live by rules that seem to us to be reasonably fair. We'll often talk about not wanting to hurt each other, for instance. But they are rules that we've made up, and when they no longer suit us they are disposable. What's more, we can't even agree amongst ourselves about what those rules should be.

So, as we've already seen, we'll look at a rule like not indulging in sexual immorality and might well agree with it. But, when we realize that when the Bible talks about sexual immorality it's referring to not having sex outside of the context of marriage, some of us are horrified. It seems so repressive! We decide instead to adopt our own, less stringent rules. Even then, despite our best intentions (even if we keep to the rules that we've created), We're well aware that we have hurt other people, and we've been hurt ourselves due to our behaviour.

The whole area of our sexual behaviour is just one in which it is clearly shown that we have failed to live in the way God intends us to. We've missed the mark; we've sinned. For most of us, we're only too aware of the fact. Now we know that sin can be defined as failing to live by God's rules, we're conscious that we are, after all, sinners. And that obviously gets in the way of our relationship with God. It has to, when we're playing different games, let alone adopting different rules.

Even though we've seen that the Bible describes the way that we've abandoned God as adultery, he still wants to have a relationship with us. But for us to enjoy the relationship with God that we were created for, something has to be done about how we've messed things up and tried to do them in our own way. We can't do a lot to erase the past, as we were saying when we were talking about the ways we've made a mess of our sex lives. That's where Jesus comes in. He offers to forgive us and grant us a new start in life as we turn around and start living in the way that he prescribes, the way that we were designed to live.

If we aren't Christians, this can seem hard to accept. We can't believe that Jesus would want anything to do with us.

Tragically, Kurt Cobain seemed to have got hold of this idea. In the *Unplugged* performance that Nirvana recorded for MTV, they played an old song by The Vaselines. It was an amended old hymn, newly entitled 'Jesus doesn't want me for a sunbeam'. The song goes on to give the reason that Jesus wouldn't want the singer for a sunbeam: 'Sunbeams are not made like me.'

Presumably Kurt identified strongly enough with the sentiments of the song to record it for the world-wide consumption of MTV viewers. Somewhere and somehow Kurt had picked up the impression that Jesus is only interested in the good people of the world, and that he couldn't possibly have any use for those on the margins, those who don't look as respectable as the ones who go to church. It's a lie that a lot of people have swallowed, and unfortunately many of our churches have added to this impression. Because church often appears to be for nice, respectable, middle-class people, there are a huge bunch of people who feel they don't fit in and they are alienated as a result. Consequently, too many buy into thinking that Jesus can't be interested in them.

It is a lie. Jesus was given a hard time by the religious authorities for hanging out with the undesirables in society. They thought it was scandalous that he ate meals with 'sinners'. Jesus had to point out to these respected religious leaders that this was the very reason that he was there. He was there for the people who needed him, whether they were considered respectable or not.[3]

That means you and me, however sophisticated we may, or may not, be as sinners. We don't need telling that we haven't lived up to the exacting standards that are laid out in the Bible.

While we can't do a lot to help ourselves, Jesus has done something about it. As Paul points out in his letter to the Romans, although we certainly don't deserve another chance, 'You see, at just the right time, when we were still powerless, Christ died for the ungodly. Very rarely will anyone die for a righteous man, though for a good man someone might possibly dare to die. But God demonstrates his own love for us in this: While we were still sinners Christ died for us.'[4]

The kind of love described here isn't a weak sentimental one. It's the kind of *agape* love that we discussed earlier, the tough unconditional love that we heard about when we discussed how we should love one another. In trying to love like that, we're seeking to love as God loves us. And his love is so deep that Jesus demonstrated it in a bloody, painful death, nailed to a tree.

Jesus doesn't wait for us to become good and respectable churchgoers before he does something about our situation. He's dealt with it already, and if we repent, turn our lives around and give them over to him as we follow him, the slate is wiped clean and we are able to start again.

It all seems too good to be true, doesn't it? We're brought up in a culture where we understandably distrust anyone who seems to offer such easy answers. Jesus' offer is straightforward. He offers us forgiveness if we turn around and repent. It's straightforward enough, but it isn't easy. Living in the way that God would have us live can be exceptionally hard sometimes – because it's the opposite to the way that most people live. But if you make that decision to become a Christian and live God's way, you can be sure that he'll help you when things are tough. That's true of the way we go about doing relationships God's way, as with any other area of life.

We have a great number of decisions to make with regard to our relationships with one another. Who do we go out with? What kind of friendship do we offer to those close to us? How do we handle our sexuality outside of marriage? Are we prepared to commit ourselves to a partner for life? These are huge questions that confront us. We must make careful choices.

The largest question we will ever face is whether we are prepared to accept that we've got things wrong, lived life our own way, and paid no attention to God. Jesus offers us a way back to God, the only way. Accepting that he has done everything necessary to re-establish that relationship with God is the way for us to be forgiven the past and to be able to embrace the future. It's the most important decision you'll ever have to make. Please, choose very carefully.

notes

1. talking about my generation

1. Jonathan Freedland, 'Welcome to the 90s', *Elle*, September 1994.
2. *Melody Maker*, 17 December 1994.
3. William Mahedy and Janet Bernardi, *A Generation Alone* (IVP [USA], 1994).
4. Douglas Coupland, *Generation X* (Abacus, 1992).

2. so lonely

1. Statistics quoted in the *Guardian*, 27 March 1996.
2. Genesis 1:26–27.
3. Perhaps the clearest reference to the Trinity is when Jesus commands his followers to go and make disciples throughout the world, '... baptising them in the name of the Father and of the Son and of the Holy Spirit' (Matthew 28:19). Also see John 14:26; 15:26; 2 Corinthians 13:14; 1 Peter 1:2.
4. John 1:1–3.
5. John 1:14.
6. 'Dance Away', by Roxy Music.
7. Survey published by Mintel in March 1996.
8. Acts 2:42–47.

3. i'll be there for you

1. 'Cartoon Emily' by Steve Ayers, in *End of an Error* (UCCF, 1994).
2. Matthew 26:37.
3. Roy McCloughry, *Men and Masculinity* (Hodder and Stoughton, 1991).
4. Quoted in *Third Way*, October 1996.
5. 1 Corinthians 13:4–7.

4. is she really going out with him?

1. Exodus 3:1–4.

2. For example, Exodus 15:13 talks of God leading and guiding the people he has redeemed; the psalmists often asked for guidance (Psalms 25:5; 31:3; 43:3; 48:14 *etc.*); and the prophet Isaiah proclaims that 'The LORD will guide you always' (Isaiah 58:11).

3. In Genesis 48:15, Jacob describes God as being his shepherd 'all my life'; the psalmist famously records this facet of God's character in Psalm 23; and there are a number of other references throughout the Bible.

4. For example, the psalmist praises God 'who counsels me' (Psalm 16:7).

5. Psalm 68:5 describes God as a father to the fatherless and a defender of widows; Isaiah 64:8 declares, 'Yet, O LORD, you are our Father'; and Jesus makes numerous references to God as Father.

6. It must be said that trusting our feelings is not always the best way to work out what we should and shouldn't do. Perhaps this is nowhere more true than in working out whether we should marry someone who, presumably, we have some strong feelings for anyway!

7. For example, Matthew 10:29–30.

8. Matthew 7:9–11; Luke 11:11–13.

9. The whole homosexuality debate is a long one and separate from the purpose of this book, but if you want to read further on this issue, *Straight and Narrow?* by Thomas Schmidt (IVP, 1995) is a good place to start.

10. Adultery is explicitly forbidden in the Ten Commandments (Exodus 20:14; Deuteronomy 5:18), as well as being warned against throughout the Bible, especially in Jesus' teaching (*e.g.* Matthew 5:27–28; Mark 10:1–12; Luke 16:18; John 8:3–11).

11. See Matthew 5:32, but evangelicals disagree on this subject. Some argue that a dispensation to divorce means that the divorced person is free to remarry.

12. 1 Corinthians 7:39–40; 2 Corinthians 6:14.

13. 2 Corinthians 6:14.
14. This is an issue concerning going out with people who are not Christians. I am not advocating that 'mixed marriages' should be dissolved (see 1 Corinthians 7:12–13).

5. everyone else is doing it so why can't we?

1. These are genuine headlines from the covers of randomly selected women's magazines.
2. These too are genuine headlines, taken from the covers of randomly selected men's magazines.
3. Drs Ruth Westheimer and Louis Lieberman, *Dr Ruth's Guide to Erotic and Sensuous Pleasures* (Robson, 1992).
4. This statistic is quoted in Mike Starkey, *God, Sex and Generation X* (Triangle, 1997), p. 47.
5. Unless otherwise noted, all the statistics used in this book are from the questionnaire that I carried out.
6. Only a small percentage of students (14%) said that they didn't know what the Bible teaches about sex and relationships. Most of those who said they knew, however, were unable to define 'fornication' (see footnote 14 below), which demonstrates less of an understanding than is claimed.
7. Genesis 1:27.
8. Matthew 19:4–6 and Mark 10:8; 1 Corinthians 6:16 and Ephesians 5:31.
9. Exodus 20:14; Deuteronomy 5:18.
10. Matthew 5:27–28.
11. Male students who were asked about their personal struggles in a different survey in 1996 – this one being among young Christian leaders – recorded that their biggest problems are: 1. the way girls dress; 2. masturbation; 3. images on film/video; 4. not having a girlfriend; and 5. explicit magazines. These replies exactly mirrored those in a similar survey in 1991. Female students also recorded that masturbation and images on film and video were among their hardest struggles.

12. Deuteronomy 24:1.
13. 1 Corinthians 7:15.
14. In the case of defining 'fornication' for instance, 40% offered no definition or admitted that they could not define it. In addition to this, 14% thought it was simply the act of sexual intercourse, and 10% had various other mistaken ideas.
15. *The Collins English Paperback Dictionary*, 1986.
16. Paul uses this phrase in nearly all his letters, so presumably sexual immorality isn't a new problem in the church, see especially 1 Corinthians 5 and 6.
17. Galatians 5:19–23.
18. 'Frostbites … A Man's Woman', from Canterbury Christ Church College's student magazine, 7 May 1996.

6. like a virgin
1. Both of these quotes are taken from Tim Stafford's book *Sexual Chaos* (IVP, 1993), p. 16.
2. Matthew 5:27–28.
3. For instance, while only four out of 132 students surveyed thought it was OK to have sex before marriage, 30 admitted that they had broken that boundary. At the same time, while 23% thought it was acceptable to draw the line at heavy petting, 60% had broken that boundary and engaged in either mutual masturbation, oral sex or genital intercourse.
4. 'Sin' can be defined as falling short of God's standards.
5. Genesis 2:24; Ephesians 5:31.

7. just like starting over
1. When asked whether there was an older person in church to whom they would feel free to talk about personal relationships and sexuality, less than half (43%) thought that there was.
2. I'm not talking here about people who have been involuntarily involved in sexual activity against their will. Such

people who have been harmed by a person imposing their will on them sexually often feel deep guilt and shame, but they shouldn't. If this has happened to you, you need to know that what happened was *not* your fault. You may think that you are in some way to blame because you feel guilty, but you cannot always trust your feelings. Forgive a crass example. You may have stolen a sum of money and not feel guilty about it in the least. It doesn't alter the fact that you are guilty – you did it. The way you *feel* about it doesn't make any difference. If you have been forced into sexual acts against your will, you are in no way the guilty party, however much you might *feel* that you are. Remember the definition that we found of fornication: '*voluntary* sexual intercourse outside marriage'. If this is an issue for you, then you will naturally have a very different view of sex from the one described in this book. You will probably find it very difficult to accept the Bible's view that sex is a gift from God, and you might feel unable to accept that it can ever be enjoyed. If so, you'd be wise to talk to someone of seniority within your church who should be able to put you in touch with someone who will be able to help you to work through how you feel about what has happened to you.

3. See 1 Peter 1:15–16. In the context of talking about being self-controlled, Peter urges the churches to be holy.
4. Luke 15:2.
5. Luke 15:3–32.
6. Luke 15:10.
7. Matthew 9:12–13.
8. 1 John 1:8–9.

8. let's stick together
1. These findings are taken from Robin Skinner and John Cleese, *Families and How to Survive them* (Cedar, 1983), pp. 66–67.
2. In *Life* (supplement to the *Observer*), 25 February 1996, and *The Independent Magazine*, 24 February 1996.

3. Between 1971 and 1990, the divorce rate in Britain rose from 73,000 to 153,000 couples.

4. Quoted in *Life*, 24 November 1996, from *UK Household Survey 1989*.

5. *Life*, 25 February 1996.

6. The Alternative Service Book 1980.

7. 1 Corinthians 13:4–8a, in Eugene H. Peterson, *The Message* (NavPress, 1995).

8. Ephesians 5:22–24.

9. John Stott, *The Message of Ephesians* (IVP, 1979), p. 219.

10. *Ibid.*, p. 225.

11. Ephesians 5:25.

12. Ephesians 5:21.

13. Kaye Wellings *et al.*, *Sexual Behaviour in Britain* (Penguin, 1994), quoted in Elaine Storkey, *The Search for Intimacy* (Hodder and Stoughton, 1995), p. 172.

14. 1 Corinthians 7:1, 8–9, 28.

15. Researched by Professor Howard Markman of the University of Denver, Colorado, and quoted in *Life*, 24 November 1996.

16. 1 Corinthians 7:32–35.

17. 2 Corinthians 11:23–28.

18. Gordon MacDonald, *Leadership*, vol. 13 no. 4, p. 69.

9. from despair to where?

1. An example of this is found in Hosea 1:2.

2. See Genesis 2:15 – 3:24 for the whole story.

3. For an example of this type of exchange, see Luke 15.

4. Romans 5:6–8.

Friends, Helpers, Lovers
The early years of marriage

IAN & RUTH COFFEY

For two people a whole new life has begun. With confetti down their necks, a rented flat and eyes only for each other, they grasp one of the greatest gifts God has ever given – marriage.

Will they live happily ever after? Will they grow more and more in love, have two fine children and a second honeymoon in Paris? Will their golden wedding photo in the local newspaper confirm that they were 'meant for each other'?

Or is there more to it than that?

In this wise and practical book, Ian and Ruth Coffey point the way to building a strong and lasting marriage. They cover a wide range of issues including good communication, building a home, developing a relationship with God as a couple, second marriages and non-Christian spouses.

Ian and Ruth have been married for over twenty years and have four children. They have a wide experience of counselling others in the area of marriage and the family, both in the UK and abroad.

192 pages   *'B' format*

Inter-Varsity Press